To: Be[illegible] M[illegible]gan

Trust Life! It's helping you!

I Am Love

Challenge yourself!

work on you!

This is your Life!

I Am Love

The Application of Healing

Tyler & Corey McEnroe

NEW • EARTH
CONNECT

Cover illustration and design by Tyler Russell

To learn more about New Earth Connect and discover your numbers,
visit http://newearthconnect.com.

Books published by New Earth Connect may be ordered through booksellers or by contacting:

New Earth Connect
162 Heatherwood Dr
Brookfield, CT 06804

http://newearthconnect.com

ISBN: 978-1-4951-6025-7

Printed in the United States of America

Table of Contents

Preface

January 1st, 2010 marked the beginning of a five-year process of conscious evolution on this planet called the Great Span. When this process began, Tyler and Corey McEnroe found themselves lost and highly engaged in the egocentric ways of our planet.

Growing up in the small town of Millbrook, NY, these two brothers were constantly surrounded by team-oriented situations. Their mother was the daughter of a local entrepreneur, and their father was a basketball coach and son of a farmer. By nature they have always looked for the best in others and have always treated them as equals no matter what backgrounds they came from.

In 2010 these two brothers stumbled across consciousness and the power of their thoughts. As they learned the fundamental aspects of awareness, they began to recognize that much of the information was sporadic and was not comprehensive. Corey and Tyler began making connections and noticing that everything in our reality is perceived as being separate, while in reality, everything is connected.

Over the course of the next five years, the brothers developed a system of energy navigation that helps people expand their awareness of who they really are. They have also expanded many concepts, bringing light to information that has not been exposed to the general public.

Corey and Tyler believe that, with this newfound awareness, we as a collective society can make the necessary changes to bring about a worldwide revolution of positivity and awareness for all. These two brothers, along with many others, have dedicated their lives to expanding the intentions of human beings here on Earth away from capital gain and into a fully abundant reality. This endeavor will be continuously modified and changed for its improvement.

The Great Span concluded on December 31st, 2014, ushering in a time in human evolution in which all individuals will begin to question the way our world is structured and seek a more positive reality for everybody on Earth.

New Earth Connect is a movement that represents the younger generation. It believes in breaking the barriers of our world that keep us from truly understanding who we are and why we are here.

This book will help us heal ourselves and discover how to utilize love to its fullest potential. The system of energy known as the Code to Your Soul (CTYS) will act as the most significant aspect of the awakening process. It will identify each individual's birth-given energy while also presenting the tools to understand how we connect with one another on an energetic level. This will inevitably heal our planet one person at a time through a natural transition away from individual power into collective abundance.

Part I:
I Am Love

The Unveiling

As time continues to take its course here on planet Earth, our collective consciousness within our physical reality remains conditioned, separate, and trapped in a state of fear and confusion. In essence, we have been taught specific thought patterns that prevent us from understanding our true potential as human beings.

From a young age we learn to see the world from a very narrow perspective, one that prevents us from seeing our own true inherent values as human beings, and from seeing the value in those around us. These thought patterns are deeply ingrained in the way that we perceive the world and cause us to see differences in human value based on race, sex, appearance, and social class.

These patterns of thinking also cause us to see ourselves as separate from our communities, creating an egocentric core value system in which we are not working together to empower the community as a whole, but are only looking out for ourselves. We believe that success is in limited supply, therefore, in order to succeed we must compete against one another to get to the top.

We have been conditioned to forget that we are all connected, that we are always affecting one another, and that we have the potential to work together to empower one another in a society in which we all prosper together. This infrastructure of our society has been gradually developed by a worldwide organization that we know as the 1%, Illuminati, or whatever high council name you may have heard.

The 1st amendment, freedom of speech, promotes a great deal of confusion because it allows for information to be placed into our collective reality with no regard for truth or objectivity. In other words, we have the freedom to speak freely, but this leaves room for manipulation. The conditioning goes so deep into the way that our minds function that in reality we are not free. This belief that we are free also causes a lack of questioning the system. These higher conglomerates have created a vision of how society experiences emotions and reality, and have manifested this vision by creating an infrastructure that supports it.

Energy generates into our reality in a collection of individual, but deeply connected, entities that we know as plants, animals, and of course humans. Humans have been given a rare state of existence that allows us to create opportunities through free will. Free will is our freedom to make our own decisions and create our realities working in conjunction with the laws of the universe.

Humans, for the last couple thousand years, have used this free will energy to create a hierarchy that drives humanity into social classes, placing different levels of value on each individual. This creates a perceived separation of human beings on a massive scale when in reality, all human beings are connected to one another. It's important for us to remember that the true, inherent value of all human beings is unconditional and is not dependent on these categories that we have created to separate ourselves from one another.

We have been conditioned from a very young age, especially in the United States, to believe that we are here to compete with our peers in order to separate the educated and the sharp from the hard-working and ignorant. As we grow up through our education system, we are judged and categorized. By the time we reach high school, most individuals have a pretty good idea of whether or not they are on the track to higher education based on how they were categorized throughout the school systems. The real question is: how do we continue to place these values on our community members and allow them to dictate the way we treat each other?

In some cases, we are taught to take pride in our heritage and beliefs, and in other cases, we are taught to be ashamed of our culture, that we are inherently less valuable as human beings because of it. Politics, entertainment, sports, education, and religion are other tools that are used to program us to believe that each person will fall into a faction or category that is judged through their actions and their appearance. Separation is a natural occurrence that as a collective we do not grasp, yet it is simply due to over and under valuing of who is better and worse.

We are now going to break down how our society influences and manipulates how we create our collective reality through the fundamentals of energy. Understanding that this is our perspective of how energy is being misused, we do not place blame on any particular group of people because all of us are expanding our awareness every day, and we can emphasize with individuals on all levels of awareness. We are all a part of this society together and, therefore, we all have a responsibility to create something that is more productive together, rather than placing blame on one group of people and initiating even more separation.

In order to create collective change, we must step outside of our comfort zones. To step outside of our comfort zones, we must chisel away at our fear of being judged by those around us. This is because the steps that must be taken in order for change to occur will be outside of what is commonly accepted as the societal norm.

Our challenge here on Earth is to reveal who we are. By doing that, comfort zones will have no choice but to break. The program that needs to be broken is the desire to focus outside of ourselves, because in truth, the main focus is ourselves.

Our reality is set up in a way that influences us to find outlets outside of ourselves to grab onto and direct us away from truly understanding who we are. We latch onto these outlets and then become dependent on the energy that they give us. We must focus on attaching to our energy and gaining strength from inside of ourselves and not allowing outside influences to continue to dictate who we are and who we become.

We must learn to cultivate relationships of love with ourselves, to truly comprehend our value as human beings and, from there, create the life that we choose through self-discipline and working with the laws of the universe.

Self-reflection is a huge medium through which we can begin to cultivate this. We must question our thought patterns, continuously asking ourselves why we are thinking the way that we are thinking. From there, we can start to unmask ourselves from these layers that we have developed, revealing our true selves, untainted by these unproductive thought patterns that teach us to hate ourselves and to hate those around us. Once we do this, we can begin to see clearly, see our own values and see the value in all human beings on this planet.

Collective Creation

Gaining the awareness how we collectively create our reality will be the first step in awakening humanity. This knowledge can give everybody the opportunity to develop enhanced senses by understanding how each of us processes thoughts. This perception will naturally increase our abilities to sense the energies of those around us.

Combining our understanding of Zodiacs, chakras, elements, lifecycles, relationships, and the levels of energy within our vortices will allow us to utilize our minds and develop to our fullest potential.

We now have the ability to find less stress and more balance within our daily lives, increasing our peace and happiness. With this awareness we have also discovered how it actually connects to the ancient Mayan Calendar of Evolution. Our society has overlooked this calendar for a reason, and in the following passages we will discuss this.

At this point in time, it is apparent that the world did not end on December 21, 2012, as experts predicted it would, according to their interpretation of the Mayan calendar. In fact, the Mayan calendar actually had concluded already on October 28th, 2011.

What the media neglected to tell the public was that the Mayans had multiple calendars, one that tracked the physical movement of the stars (the Gregorian), one that determined the birth-given energy in which you chose to incarnate (the Tun calendar), and one that tracked the evolution of our universe's collective consciousness, and that's the one that we're going to talk about.

The last of these calendars began nearly 16.4 billion years ago and was broken into 9 levels, all of which presented our universe with a tool for conscious development.

We will now break down these 9 levels by showing you the tools they gave us and how they relate to the energy of the number cycle.

The first cycle was the **Cellular cycle**, and its tool was action/reaction. Science would call this the Big Bang, or the beginning of creation at its smallest point through the structure of atoms. The result in evolution was the first single-cell organism on our planet nearly 1.26 billion years ago.

This was the first cycle, and it relates to the energy of 1, creativity and confidence, because it was the creation of the basic structure of all living things, therefore, giving life confidence to expand.

The second cycle was the **Mammalian cycle**, and its tool was stimulus response. This is when cells began to clump together and started to produce physical life forms. The result in evolution was the first live birth.

The number 2 is represented by cooperation and balance, as it is reflective of atoms beginning to cooperate with each other in order to begin creating structure and balance within physical life.

The third cycle is the **Familial cycle**, and its tool was stimulus and individual response. This was when monkeys first appeared on the planet and animals were able to distinguish between families and herds through the recognition of the individual.

This works with the energy of 3, expression and sensitivity, because it marked the beginning of individual expression and the sensitivity of being connected to a family.

The fourth cycle is the **Tribal cycle**, and its tool for transformation was the mind, or the ability to recognize similarities and differences. This was when the first cavemen appeared on Earth and the human being began its process of evolution. The result was the mind's ability to not just act, but make decisions.

This relates to the energy of 4, stability and process, because it marked the beginning of human progress on Earth, creating a foundation for human life.

The fifth cycle is known as the **Cultural cycle**, and its tool was the ability to reason. This is when different cultures began to form on Earth and their basis for existence was shared reasoning. The result in evolution was agriculture and religions or belief systems, which created a reason to live.

This relates to the energy of 5, freedom and discipline, because shared reasoning creates collective discipline. In addition, a sense of freedom to create different groups based on preferred religion was created, along with the ability to produce our own food.

The sixth cycle is known as the **National cycle**, and its tool was law. This is when the first nation was established when the upper and lower Nile communities came together through the marriage of the prince and princess to create Egypt. The result in evolution was the ability to write, which created human-sanctioned consequences through right and wrong, crime and punishment, and fear and love.

This relates to the energy of 6, vision and acceptance, by creating a vision of society that is based on law, which inevitably creates a system of worth and value for each individual.

The seventh cycle is known as the **Planetary cycle**, and its tool was power. This was the beginning of the Industrial Revolution when machines were created and they started to do work for man. In addition, the expansion of chemical combustion was discovered in addition to scientific power. The result in evolution was the birth of the Internet, manifesting a globally-connected consciousness.

This relates to the energy of 7, trust and openness. You can see this in the expansion of scientific discovery and a presentation in our society with an energy of trust in the powers that exist. During this era, members of society did not necessarily question the status quo.

The eighth cycle is known as the **Galactic cycle**, and the tool was ethics. This era took place from 1999 to 2011, and was clearly exemplified through all of the unethical behavior that took place in major businesses. Examples of this include Enron in 2004, insider trading in 2008, and the child molestation charges against Jerry Sandusky in 2011.

The result in evolution was the idea that our system of life and the way our society functions may not be as ethical as we once believed it to be.

This aligns with the energy of 8, abundance and recognition, because it allowed society to start to recognize that the abundance in our world is being misused and overpowered by a minority. This has now manifested into the 1% versus 99% movement.

The ninth and final cycle is known as the **Universal cycle**, and its tool was co-creation. This took place in the year of 2011, and it raised awareness about the lack of equality that exists in this world, especially in the United States. This energy is what fueled Occupy Wall Street and the desire for the 99% to begin to challenge the powers that control society.

This is aligned with the energy of 9, wisdom and integrity, because it has brought the integrity of our society to the collective awareness. It revealed that our society does not hold very high integrity, and we realized that change must occur on this planet.

After following the conscious evolution of our planet, we are brought back to 0, and to the expansion of enormous gifts that have been hidden from us for thousands of years.

Today, each and every one of us is being presented with the opportunity to understand who we truly are, and why we are here on this planet. Now that we have gone through all nine cycles and have a greater understanding of how energy works within our lives, we have the necessary tools to understand ourselves in relation to our birth-given energies.

This aligns with the energy of 0 that possesses inner gifts, as we are now able to access the gift of self-awareness, which can drastically assist the resolution of conflict that exists on our planet.

Your personal point of view and moment of physical incarnation has a time and place in which you manifested your physical experience. When your awareness of your purpose on this planet is established, your birth-given energies can merge with your passions in order to put you in sync with your personal divine life purpose.

Luck, coincidence, and chance are all falsifications of the mind that have been created in order to separate us from the natural harmony and synchronicity of life.

We are all meant to align with our divine paths, and it is time to discover this by peeling back the layers of conditioning that we have developed by living in this society since birth.

The work that we have to do on ourselves individually may not be easy. However, when this journey is embarked upon, a newfound sense of self-love will begin to develop.

Once we are working on this consistently, the stress-filled lives that we create today will be an experience of the past. We will use the acronym "AAA" as a metaphor for how we can go about breaking down these layers of ourselves that we have developed. In essence, we are breaking our spirits down.

AAA stands for:

Acknowledge, Accept, and Allow.

When we can acknowledge the things that we hold onto that cause us pain, that distract us from getting to know ourselves, then we are able to identify what exactly we need to work on.

These issues derive from different experiences that have occurred in our lives that impact us greatly both emotionally and energetically. For example, if someone has a traumatic experience in his childhood, that experience has impacted the way that he sees the world and sees himself.

Many of these experiences happen in our childhoods because throughout our childhoods we are developing our perspectives of the world and the way that we see ourselves in relation to the world. Many of these perceptions that we have developed are not productive and do not serve us. We hold them deep in our core ethos energetically.

Once we are able to identify what these perceptions are, in addition to specific experiences that impacted us negatively, we are able to navigate them and release them while re-working those perceptions into something more productive and truthful.

Our system, called the Code to Your Soul (CTYS), will be a huge tool to help in this endeavor. This system gives our logical minds a platform from which to point out certain issues inside of ourselves, as well as giving us the tools to optimize on our strengths.

From there, we are able to identify why certain things have happened to us throughout our lives. This will allow us to begin the process of accepting the past for what it was, while moving through these feelings without creating blockages. This will give us the personal strength and ability to allow these layers that are not serving us to be released.

Change inside of ourselves will certainly not be easy, but we must first and foremost let go of all of the mistakes that we have made and tragedies that we have experienced by acknowledging them as part of previous versions of ourselves.

Breaking down the layers of conditioning that we have developed by living in this society is certainly a challenge, but for us to create collective change, we must support one another through this process and focus on the changes that we need to make in order to be one with ourselves and with the universe.

Karma

Karma is the universal law that the energy released into the universe will be returned. Therefore, if the energy that you release into the universe is love, you will receive love, and if you release negativity into the universe, negativity will be returned to you.

This universal law is something that we all experience. Whether good or bad, it's a constant part of our energetic reality. Good karma is drawn to you when you go out of your way to help others, when you live from a standpoint of high integrity, and when you keep your thoughts positive.

Negative karma draws to you largely through three separate, but often connected, energies to include hatred, delusion, and lust.

The return of karma whether good or bad comes in a variety of fashions. For example, if you involve yourself in delusion and lust, the return of that negative energy may reflect in a number of issues with the law, a problem with addiction, a physical illness, a loss of employment, or anything that may not be working out to your benefit.

It is possible that readers are saying to themselves, well life was a disaster for me from the beginning, I didn't create that karma. This is true. However, our souls carry karma with them from our past life experiences. Personal awareness of how energy is reciprocated through your decision-making can and will drastically help you decipher whether or not your karma is functioning positively or negatively.

As we address the negative we will first discuss how hatred projects outwardly, reflecting that pain back into your personal energetic field. Understanding that what you project is what you reflect, these negative energies can return to you in a multitude of ways.

The word "hate" alone carries a tremendous amount of negative energy. Just the pure use of this word carries bad karma, even if the intent of it is not in line with the low vibration of this word.

One of the most powerful types of hatred is discrimination, especially when it's driven toward others based on race, sex, beliefs, or sexuality. The human race does not control what heritage we are or what our sexual preference is or what belief system conditions us, as we are born into those categories. These are variables that are uniquely ours. They are gifts to our souls for existing and, therefore, there is no reason to judge others or try and categorize who is better and who is worse.

When you transmit negative energy toward others based on these inherent qualities, it draws the worst form of negativity toward yourself and those who are close to you. Not only do you bring negative karma to yourself when you engage in this type of discrimination, but you perpetuate a cycle of oppression that is long ingrained into our society's infrastructure. You contribute to the hatred an individual has for himself by engaging in discrimination because eventually that individual will internalize this idea that he is less valuable because of his or her race, sex, or sexuality after a lifetime of being taught that this is the case.

Hatred has been hurting this planet's collective consciousness for thousands of years. Bringing this awareness to our own thought process and sharing that with the collective will naturally begin to heal and help transition our projections away from this energy.

The next type of negative karma is the creation of delusion. Everybody has indulged in this energy a multitude of times because we are conditioned to look out for ourselves first and foremost, manifesting the use of delusion into our reality. Clearly the art of lying is the number one culprit of delusion. Whether it is a subtle lie or a constant series of lies that affect you every day, this aspect of delusion will affect your vibration in negative forms. We lie because, in that moment, we're not necessarily concerned about how the other person will be affected by the dishonestly. We're more concerned with ourselves. Honesty can be a challenging concept to maintain because sometimes it's easier to avoid conflict with a "white lie."

The negative karma accumulated from small lies may not be large individually. However, over time they become constant, which can begin to affect others in negative ways. One of the most powerful forms of delusion stems from sexual relationships and the energy of attachment that comes with it. Because sexual energy is sacred and very powerful, it can be the gateway to our personal spiritual awakenings. When we use delusion within our sexual relationships, whether it be cheating or misleading our partners about our true feelings, we receive a tremendous amount of negativity.

No matter what form of delusion you may project, it is important to find the strength to clear all the delusion that has been created. No matter what the outcome may be, you're only hurting yourself by continuing to live in a world of lies.

Lust is an energy that we attach to primarily because it is something that makes us feel good about ourselves while also acting as a distraction from our problems. Whether it be an over-indulgence in work, gambling, food, drugs, or sex, it is something that must be acknowledged and then navigated. Lust tends to be a direct result of the misuse of delusion.

It is important to realize that when you have these urges that reflect as addictions, they are created by the mind, and are then controlled by your will to continue to feed them or to ignore them. The mind continues to give us reasons to continue down the path of lust because it becomes a consistent energy that builds repetition within our everyday creations. These indulgences can also offer an escape from looking inside of ourselves and confronting painful or difficult emotions or thoughts. Self-control and the desire to change are the keys to transmuting your personal karma to a positive form.

When karma is working in positive forms it is a wonderful experience, and life can be simple and enjoyable. One of the biggest ways to draw positive vibrations toward you is by granting kindness to others and treating everybody as equals.

Everybody on this planet has gifts and qualities that are extremely unique and, because of this, we can't compare ourselves to one another and see ourselves as more or less valuable based on skill sets or talents in certain areas. If we all can become more giving and more unified as a collective, the natural karma for all of us will start manifesting a reality that is more positive than negative.

Unfortunately at this moment in time we live in a world of separation that is over-indulged in negative karma on a daily basis. As individuals we cannot worry about the actions of others because we have no control over them. We do have control over our own actions. The more people that produce positive karma, the greater the opportunity for world-wide collective change.

Religion

Religion is one of the most controversial and sensitive topics that exists in our culture today simply because it separates individuals into different belief systems that all have the same general messages: the belief in a higher power, unexplainable spiritual events of the past, and life after death. Many religions condition us to believe that we exist in one physical life and that when that lifetime is over, we will experience either heaven or hell in our afterlife based on our actions this lifetime.

The truth of the matter is that we are and always have been souls first and temporary physical bodies second. Death is only an illusion that religion has distinguished as an unknown transformation of self. This concept of creating a reality where all individuals fear death leads us to believe that this is our only opportunity to live.

Before we continue to discuss religion it is important to first understand how dimensions of consciousness work from the 3rd to the 5th dimensions.

We physically exist in the 3rd dimension where time is linear. We have 24 hours in a day, 7 days in a week, 52 weeks in a year, and so on. Either way there is a constant structure of time upon which everybody on the planet agrees.

When you dream, your consciousness enters the 4th dimension where time is no longer linear. When you experience situations of déjà vu here in the present, it happens because your consciousness has experienced a similar event in the dream realms that end up occurring in a future physical timeline.

In the 4th dimension we are also capable of consciously experiencing events and interacting with spirits who have already passed away here on Earth. From personal experience I have had two very close friends pass on at a young age who continue to communicate with me in the dreams realms. This not only aided my healing process of losing two close friends, but it also showed me that death is truly an illusion and that we are all naturally divine beings that chose to be part of the human 3rd dimensional earth experience.

The 5th dimension is what some may understand to be heaven. It's where the soul makes the conscious decision to be entirely of-love. Of-love is the state of consciousness in which the spirit frees itself of the ego, and therefore embodies the frequency of love without any interference from lower vibrational thoughts, emotions, or energies. Because the 5th dimension is all love, when an individual passes away, she enters the 4th dimension where the spirit has the option to remain and create a reality of hell for herself in the lower dimensions or pass through the gateway to the 5th dimension or the heavens. Either way it is a reality that your soul will create for itself based on how you conditioned your mind throughout your life here on Earth.

When you enter back into the 5th dimension, you have the option to continue fully of-love or reincarnate back on Earth or potentially even another planet that harbors life. Regardless, your soul is conscious and will always be given a choice.

The Bible and the story of Jesus Christ is the main focus of most Western religions. Jesus spread a message that all were created in God's image and that we are all divine. This is the root of what drives people to internalize and believe the messages in the Bible. What most do not see or understand is that Jesus told a story and then was crucified for his ability to influence others. As this story travelled from village to village, the people in power at the time took notice of how strong his influence truly was.

King James recognized that he could manipulate Jesus' message in order to control the masses through belief. Taking the positive lifestyle, the idea of life after death and the concept of heaven with which Jesus so profoundly influenced people, King James created a duality, or a concept of hell and sin. He then told through Jesus' story that sin was a real thing, that you can and will commit sin, and that it's okay as long as you pray to God, admit your sins, and ask for forgiveness. This manifested a free pass for individuals to engage in negative karmic activities.

Prayer is really just a conscious intention that we drive toward one entity "God" rather than just releasing it into the collective consciousness or universe. Those thoughts hold the same weight, but they are just manipulated by the belief that one "super-human" is responsible for answering our requests. The truth of the matter is that the manifestation of a so-called request or prayer will be fulfilled by your karmic energy and your ability to consciously create a positive outcome that doesn't overtake the free will of another individual.

For example, if an individual prays for a woman to date him, no matter how clean that individual's karma is that woman has free will and, therefore, those manifestations can affect her but only at her will. We must acknowledge the fact that in the end she has a choice.

Prayers that provide you with personal strength to overcome adversity are mental positive reinforcing intentions that will naturally manifest this strength into your reality. Prayers usually reflect your karmic energy, and as a result, the better human you are, the more positive your intentions remain. The more positive the intentions are, the more likely it is that better fortune will manifest overtime.

Government

The government was established to organize humanity through laws, the exchange of currency, and the control of human interactions. Those in power disguise government organizations as being for the benefit of the people, especially in the United States, by giving the citizens the right to vote.

In reality, it is the 1%, or the individuals at the top of the pyramid, who influence the government because of the immense amount of money and power that they posses. This 1% owns the major corporations and, therefore, has total control of everything from our oil supply, to our education, to our medical industry, to the pharmaceutical industry, to agriculture, to the big banks. Therefore, the government has no choice but to accept influence from this group of people, and by giving the public the right to vote, an illusion is created to make the public feel as if they are in control.

We are now going to examine exactly how the USA was established from a worldwide viewpoint. When the public feels as if they are in control, the chances of uprising and questioning of the system are diminished. We will now examine the process of evolution that the US government has gone through since it was originally established.

When the USA was first discovered, the original settlers created this platform of wealth that we know as the 1% today. They arrived here establishing property ownership in three predominant cities including Boston, New York, and Jamestown.

As history developed the country began to divide itself into states and was considered "One Free Nation." This development in the country's history opened the floodgates for immigrants and the right to own slaves. Individual traveled to the United States from all over the world, as our Founding Fathers had created a document that made the immigrants feel as though they were entering a land of equal opportunity.

At the time, there was in fact equal opportunity because the infrastructure of the society was just beginning. As time proceeded, however, and the country expanded into 50 states, the idea of equality and freedom began to fade away.

As equality withered away, the illusion of freedom remained and still remains today. One of the ways in which this illusion of freedom was kept intact was through state laws that contradicted the country's laws.

Over time we continued to experience movements such as women's rights, equal opportunity for minorities, and a constant idea that productive positive changes are happening to this country.

The truth of the matter is that the original families that settled here are either part of the 1% or are financially very well off. They created a nation that was supposed to represent freedom and now is the Mecca for the conscious illusion that we experience here today.

The United States government controls every aspect of our reality whether they do it right out in the open or subliminally through marketing. Unless we make the conscious choice to think independently, the government has full control over how we think and feel. Three of the primary tactics that they use are confusion, pride, and belief.

Confusion is manifested into our reality in order to lead our personal consciousness into states of subjectiveness. The laws of freedom of speech and freedom of information are the pillars of confusion. These amendments give us the ability to publish anything we would like, and nowadays, use the world wide web to really fill our realities with confusion.

Something else that contributes to this influx of false information has to do with the way that we have been raised in our society. From a very young age we are taught to look outwardly for validation from others rather than cultivating value for ourselves and understanding our own value. Therefore, we look to other individuals such as our significant others to show us that we have value, rather than recognizing this for ourselves.

New Earth Connect created a system of numerology by conducting our own studies. The information that we received from these studies is untainted, directly from the source of human interaction. Because of this, we were able to create a system that will effectively help the human mind comprehend its personal reality. If you research numerology, you will find some consistent ideas that are based off of Pythagoras' original system.

Each individual goes out of her way to receive this validation from society, so much of the information that is released is not concerned with truth, but rather with protecting our own egos and proving ourselves within this society. For example, somebody might write a dissertation with his own biases in relation to how he wants to be perceived by society, rather than focusing on providing accurate and factual information. This naturally dilutes information and promotes confusion in whatever type of topic you may look to study.

Pride is something that we are all taught at a young age. Whether you're prideful of your heritage, where you grew up, or your personal identity within society, we are taught to be proud.

What we don't realize is that pride is something that is used to separate us from one another. When we have pride we believe that we are better than other groups of people who are not of our heritage, hometown, or whatever else we might identify with.

Our system does an incredible job of manifesting pride on a number of different levels. American pride is something that is ingrained into us since childhood starting with the idea of "I'm proud to be an American where at least I know I'm free." This drives an idea into our culture that being from the United States of America is a great honor. This idea is also used to create competition and separation state-to-state, city-to-city, and town-to-town.

On the surface this competitive culture may seem friendly, however, it aids in the manifestation of hatred and crime based on nationality or hometown.

Separation is even created through competition with sports. For example, when we were children most of us played Little League with our rival town. We most likely played on the same team until we got to high school where we were separated to play against one another. What was once a close group of friends and teammates have now turned against one another because of the competition that was created by pride. There is a good chance that we were not accepted by our respective communities if we looked at our rivals as friends because of this pride that we've developed.

Pride has guided humanity throughout history, creating separations between many people, spurring several wars and conflicts. Pride is certainly an energy that we need to let go of. We must break the barriers that separate us from one another, because in the end, we are all of equal value as human beings on this planet, and we are all souls here to experience physical form. Pride only creates negative karmic energy that is driven through hatred and its different forms of separation.

Our government is very aware of how easily influenced we are. With this knowledge, our government uses the powerful energy of belief to manipulate us all of the time. The highest level of officials are aware of this power, and with this knowledge they provide us only with information that they want us to believe and, therefore, many times leave out critical information. By withholding information and by keeping the public uninformed, it is much easier to control humanity and get us to cooperate.

For centuries these officials have given us half-truths to keep us "informed," but they don't actually zoom out and share a bigger picture with us. This is where the idea of having "classified information" comes from.

When we recognize that the government keeps information private it will strike a chord with us and allow us to realize that our government is not for the people, rather, for the control of the people. Most of the time what the government wants you to believe is not the truth. The sooner that we understand this as a collective, the sooner the stronghold on our collective consciousness can be released and shifted into something more productive.

Another role that the government plays in the control of the public is the creation of laws over civilians within a certain country, state, or town. The old saying of "laws are made to be broken" is ironically accurate. Laws take away our free will by instilling a sense of fear into the general public. This gives the government a way to control a vast majority of its civilians. Instead of following the rules to create a better environment and society, we now have individuals only following these rules out of fear of being punished.

For those who break laws, punishment is required through a public hearing. The purpose of having this public hearing is to embarrass the rule-breaker, rather than to help the individual understand the negative impact of his or her actions. With these negative motivators, we have an entire society operating from a place of fear rather than love for humanity and wanting to make the world a better place.

One of the reasons that our souls incarnate onto this planet is to learn specific lessons, to expand and to grow. Throughout our journey these lessons that we learn should be a chance for us to grow and they should not be a burden that we carry with us.

Our society places different levels of value on various groups of people depending upon how much they actually fit into the structure of society's laws. Therefore, when a law is broken we put shame on that individual, and label him as a criminal. When labeled as criminals, these individuals internalize this perceived lack of value and, therefore, they don't understand their potential to grow and heal and be positive contributions to society.

Energetically our government uses this internalized shame to keep groups of people in lower vibrations, therefore, putting them into positions in which they will continue to make mistakes and repeat a pattern of self-hatred.

Meanwhile, those who remain law-abiding citizens think they are inherently more valuable than those who have broken the laws. At the same time, they are still living exactly how the government wishes them to, in fear of losing this perceived value that they have obtained from abidingly the laws. Fear stands for False Evidence Appearing Real, which the government continues to use in order to trick our vibration one way or another into this fear.

Once you become a part of the criminal system, our society has been trained to convince your mind that something is wrong with you. For example, when you go through any probation or rehabilitation program, you take courses that require you to say out loud that you are indeed an addict or that you have extreme anger problems. Because of this, these issues begin to magnify or manifest for the individual to hold onto. Once your consciousness accepts that it does in fact possess a certain issue it will continue to create that into its reality. Once people are labeled as criminals, they rarely escape that title within society.

This is not to disregard the fact that many individuals are in fact dealing with challenges, and these challenges contribute to the reason that they have committed a crime in the first place. What is important to remember here is that every human being faces challenges of varying magnitude and, therefore, we all have the ability to empathize with these people instead of judging them.

All mistakes and challenges are a part of every soul's journey, and we must embrace them as such, learning opportunities, and help people rise past these challenges. Once we label and judge these people we limit their ability to grow and heal with every challenge that they face.

Our laws are directly influenced by the organization of the capitalist infrastructure from which our society is built. If it weren't for money, many laws wouldn't be necessary because there would be less of a motivation to commit crime. This is where we get the idiom, "money is the root of all evil."

When the US began, all the "old money" families established themselves before the immigrants arrived, they created a financial system that put them into a permanent position of power in which their families would forever be financially abundant. Now, four hundred years later, these families sit back doing whatever they please while all the descendents of the immigrants and slaves chase "the American Dream."

Equal opportunity is a false idea that is fed to the 99 percent in order to make us feel like we are getting a fair shot in life. This false feeling keeps us from questioning anything about our lives and therefore, keeps us under control.

In reality, we have anything but an equal opportunity, as we are conditioned to search for a way to fit within the confines of our society. This draws us away from discovering our true potential and purpose here on Planet Earth. In order to do this we must think differently, and think about how we can contribute to the world positively.

In reality, the majority of prescription drugs are just synthetic forms of heroin or speed. Hard drugs keep individuals at lower vibrations, as they manifest realities of pain and suffering. This not only affects the individual using drugs, but it also affects the families and friends of those users, as well any individual that they may come into contact with on a daily basis. Drugs also serve the capitalist economy by keeping police officers employed and the jails filled, bringing in millions of dollars in revenue every year to state and county governments.

The story of Rick Ross (not the rapper) serves as a prime example of how our government directly supplies drugs to the community. This man was bringing in millions of dollars worth of cocaine a week into our country in the '80s. His operation was eventually discovered, and he was convicted and sentenced to three times life in prison. He was recently released from prison because there was undeniable evidence that government officials were the ones who were supplying him with his product.

The community wanted to make a film surrounding Rick Ross's story, but the government banned the film from being created as to not blow their cover.

The government's control of drug use in this country is very important to understand because it shows you that drugs actually drive revenue, promote crime, and most importantly, aid in the creation of negative karmic realities that keep society easily manipulated.

As long as we continue to accept the system that our Founding Fathers have created, the government will continue to keep this infrastructure in place. The more we continue to learn and expand our awareness about what is truly going on, the more we will comprehend the ways in which we can start to be pioneers of a new way of living, one in which we are not following the system blindly, but operating in awareness.

It is important that we do not continue to fuel the structure of this system, but consciously make steps away from that. We can start by sharing our knowledge within our circles of friends and family. Fear is one of the only mechanisms that will prevent us from overcoming this injustice. We must remain vigilant and proactive from a place of understanding humanity's potential, rather than operating from a place of fear.

It is important for us to understand that our strength will always be in our numbers and that this system that is currently in place only works because we feed it every single day. No matter what our role may be within society, we are part of the problem simply because we are a part of this society. We are not separate.

These changes will not happen overnight, but will be something that the next generation twenty years from now will have the power to change if we all begin to start waking up to these issues now, while we are all still young and not as deeply conditioned. Choice is something every single one of us has and always will have. We should never underestimate the power of our choices.

Education

From the time we are born until our early twenties, human beings are very sensitive to information. Because we are experiencing new stimuli and are having our first encounters with new situations, this is where the formation for our belief system and consciousness develops. The leaders of our education system use this time when we are very sensitive to new information to optimize the conditioning process.

During this time our reality is separated into levels of value. Children are separated by creating competition amongst the students based on the individuals who are considered the most educated or the smartest, to the average students, down to the problem children that do not take schooling as seriously as others.

The students who score high on their tests and continue on to college are funneled right back into the system. They are labeled as products of success, promoting the idea that if you get through the system you will live a "fulfilled life" and make the best of your opportunities.

Then you also have the individuals who do not do particularly well in school that end up as blue collar workers.

Lastly, there are the people who don't make it through high school and are labeled as troubled kids. These are the individuals who usually end up fueling the crime and drug abuse categories of our society.

No matter which category you end up in, it is important to realize that this path was not something you chose, but was something that was given to you. This system creates a clear divide in perceived levels of human value based on your level of success in the education system. This blocks us from seeing our own inherent value as a human beings that is present no matter what education we may have had and no matter how society may perceive us.

When we begin schooling as small children, we are placed in classes and taught very simple ideas of sharing, reading, math, science, and history. From 1st through 6th grade the conditioning process begins, separating the children through the grading system that instantly places value on each child.

There are the stand-out children who are consistently at the top of the class, that take pride in their success. Next, we have the middle group of children who maintain a mediocre level of success and who are encouraged to do better and compete to improve to the top of the class. Lastly, we have the bottom of the class, those with learning disabilities who are placed in remedial classes, separated from the normal students and are told that they are special.

By separating children at such a young age, the conditioning begins. They start to internalize the idea that humans are not equal, and that they have different levels of value. They start to develop the idea that they must compete with their peers in order to succeed or fail, and we have no choice but to play.

When we grow older and enter junior high school and high school, new ideologies are presented within our realities.

The first is a new system of grading that ranges from A-F. The "F" within the grading system stands for failing, and because of this harsh language that is used, students who fail continue to internalize the idea that they are of less value than students who receive higher grades.

The second ideology that becomes ingrained into school students is in regard to extracurricular activities or hobbies. If you excel in a given activity or hobby at a very high level, this activity could later become your profession. A majority of this occurs within fine arts and athletics, but there are slim chances that most children will actually make it to the big leagues or as a professional artist.

Another huge aspect of school culture that contributes to the conditioning lies within social interactions and sexuality, and the separation of cliques or groupings of kids based on these perceived levels of value. For example, one group of students will gather together because they study diligently and are perceived by their classmates as being less valuable because of their interests and how they look. Another group of students might rally together because they play the same sport and are perceived as more valuable because they look and act a certain way. In addition, you may have another group of students that may come together because they have what is perceived as rough family backgrounds and are looked at as less valuable because of this.

At the beginning of our education, we are conditioned to believe that graduating from college is the most respected way to live our lives. Our friends and families drill this into our value systems, and we end up believing that with a degree we will be provided with the greatest opportunity to succeed.

The fact of the matter is that yes, this the best way to be successful within our society's infrastructure. If you take a closer look at the college system you will see that the intentions of this infrastructure are not for the sole purpose of education and the progression of society. A college education contributes to the conditioning process, while also putting a majority of college students in large amounts of debt when they graduate.

The college experience is extremely glorified within our society, especially when you attend a major university or any four-year school. First and foremost, our legal drinking age is 21, but if you attend any four-year school, underage drinking is not only allowed but highly encouraged. This party culture that is present in almost every single college gets students into the habit of learning how to manage minor addictions while at the same time being able to function and get their work done.

For those that graduate and go straight into the working force, a large majority brings some sort of destructive habit with them that is widely accepted within our society. Those who don't make it through school are normally even deeper into drug and alcohol addictions with nothing to show for it but a large debt and the same type of job they would have gotten if they never went to school in the first place.

A majority of students leave school with instant debt, which puts a tremendous amount of pressure on them to find a job in the field in which they've acquired a degree, locking them into the system indefinitely in order to sustain a career and continue to pay off their debts.

Most majors are poorly structured, pushing students to engage in a surplus of years and acquire extra credits, inevitably creating more debt for each of these students who participate in the programs, while giving the schools more income. Some majors, especially any type that has to do with science, need extensive time and training. On the other hand, there are many majors that require certain training and requisites that are really only there to fuel the funds of the school.

Education provides you with knowledge, but at the same time, the curriculum is government-controlled and is a major asset in the process of conditioning the human mind. This conditioning keeps us from truly understanding our individual and collective purposes here on Earth. System placement and levels of value amplify the self-absorbed ego to continue the process of living and dying, funneled through greed, separation and confusion. Change can only happen when we use our intelligence to see past the failures of our education system.

War

War has been a part of humanity for thousands of years. During ancient times, war was used by kings and emperors to conquer land and take ownership over large groups of people. Over time, war has evolved into something with a much more complex intention. Today, war is used for population control, financial gain, and the infiltration of negative karmic activity.

War is one of the most powerful manipulation tools that our government uses because it grabs our emotions in a way that is unique and captivating.

Population scientists worldwide have estimated that our planet will hold nearly 10 billion people by the year 2050. With such a dense population, the need for change is even more urgent.

Realistically, for us to sustain a productive lifestyle, there are very few options available. One of the options is to become a global society in which we work as a unified community, working together and thriving together. The second option is to limit the growth of our population in order to sustain this unproductive infrastructure that is in place.

War is a tactic that is used to control the population, while also creating a negative karmic imprint on humanity. The soldiers that do survive return home carrying tremendous amounts of emotional baggage that affects everybody they contact.

When you zoom out you start to see that the 1% benefits greatly from war financially. Our country prospers from our involvement in third world countries, specifically in relation to oil collection.

Once oil is acquired, it is shipped all over the country with inflated prices that are justified because the country is at war. Citizens are left with no choice but to accept these inflated prices.

In addition to these benefits from oil, our government also benefits from the sale of weapons. Ironically, many times these weapon sales are made to the very countries with whom we are at war. While we are at war with these countries we are also teaching our war tactics and giving them the tools to perpetuate this war.

In relation to population control, if we continue in the direction we are headed, what lies ahead of us in ten years is alarming. It is disheartening that the government doesn't even attempt to hide these manipulative tactics surrounding war from us. They continue this manipulation with the belief that the collective will never rise up and organize a rebellion against these injustices.

Our government has created a campaign revolving around the idea that supporting and protecting your country is an honor. The illusion of pride for our country is used against us in order to get us to support these projects that have poor agendas. For example, financial benefits and advantages are given to families who elect to protect our country.

If we believe our country is superior, we feel the need to protect it, and we actually get an ego boost of pride when we do so. Because positive emotions are related to protecting our country, we do not question the agenda of war because we are wrapped up in the emotions that we feel when we support it.

This campaign is largely used to recruit soldiers for the army. As our economy continues to struggle, more and more individuals are choosing the path of joining the military, continuing this cycle of manifesting pain and negative karma.

War is also used to continue to create enemies and pit people against one another. For example, war creates anger inside of citizens who lose their loved ones, and with this, a strong emotional connection to pride for our country is created, and the desire to defend.

Physically we may be free, but when you look at the way that we are manipulated into believing that war holds great purpose, you can see that mentally, we are not free.

Media and Marketing

We will now address the role of entertainment within the process of our society's collective conditioning.

Beginning with childhood, the media presents to us many pictures of a successful life. With these images we begin to develop an idea of what our lives "should look like." Because of this, we develop identities that are external, that we latch onto and claim as our own instead of building our identities from scratch.

We must become aware of how the media is influencing us and choose to engage with it differently, otherwise we will continue to manifest a life and identity that is false, that we have not chosen for ourselves.

Many sayings and idioms are so ingrained into the way that we think about media that we don't even realize how much the media is affecting us. One example is the saying, "don't believe everything you see on TV." This ideology causes us to mix fantasy with truth. Because this idea seems so obvious to us on a conscious level, we don't realize that subconsciously we are not taking an honest look at how much we are truly buying into and believing these images.

There is so much deception going on that we are unsure of what is truth and what is fiction. In essence, there is a fine line between what is true and what is false when it comes to the media. For example, many shows on TV are "reality shows." We are aware that much of what is presented on these shows is false, but we still hold this idea that there is a sense of truth present by the mere title of "reality show."

Another example is the correlation of steroids within the professional baseball arena. No matter how successful a player may be or how thoroughly tested he is, as a society, we will always be skeptical of whether or not this player was cheating.

We create a false sense of clarity and assuredness that we know truth from falsity because we are taught that being tricked or being looked at as a fool is embarrassing. By creating a sense of assuredness, we protect our egos from being embarrassed, but this also prevents us from continuing to question and seek truth. Ironically, by failing to question and seek truth, we are continuing to be tricked and fooled.

Another sector of our media that influences us regularly is music. Vibrations of sound are heard, internalized, and then projected into our reality. Messages hidden inside of catchy tunes stick with us, and they become thoughts, which turn into energy, which affect us on a physical level. Because of this, the music that we listen to has a huge influence on the reality that we create.

Humanity's susceptibility to sound is optimized on in a negative way in order to control the way that we think and the reality that we create. This is the reason that the music industry is controlled and used as a marketing tool that convinces humanity how to live and behave. An example of a time when this control through music really took off was in the '70s when music began to push our society toward the use of drugs.

We will now examine hip-hop culture and how its music is being used to influence the way that we think and the reality that we live in. At its roots, hip-hop music contained messages of all different kinds, and many of them were just expressions of what was already going on in society and the frustrations that the people were having. There were many messages that were also very positive, about how to spread peace and love and build community.

Once hip-hop started to gain popularity, individuals from the dominant culture saw how they could capitalize off of it and how they could control people with its messages. With this, they took different ideas from hip-hop music that they could commercialize and make money from, and amplified those ideas.

This is how hip-hop became what it is today, something that is associated with poverty, crime, gang life, drug use, gold chains, fancy cars, mistreating women and much more.

This is not in fact what hip-hop is at its roots. As Afrika Bambaataa, the grandfather of hip-hop stated, hip-hop is about "peace, unity, and having fun."

As hip-hop continued to be popularized and misappropriated, these negative messages were amplified and used to aid in the conditioning of humanity. This version of "hip-hop" glamorizes drug use, crime and much more, creating positive emotions around these types of destructive behaviors. By listening to hip-hop music so consistently, we start to internalize these negative behaviors and these positive emotions that are attached to them and, therefore, they are manifested into our reality.

In addition to hip-hop, every other music genre also has its own unique way of contributing to the conditioning process. For example, electronic dance music continues to perpetuate hard drug use in a different setting, and country music sends a message about being loyal to your country, living the "good old American way."

Discovering how much the music industry is really controlling our reality is very empowering. As awareness continues to spread, we envision talented artists all over the world using their power to influence the world in a positive way. We must break the cycle of fueling a popular culture that is harming our subconscious. We can use our awareness to consciously navigate the delusion and negativity that surrounds us. Having this awareness will strike a chord with many and, slowly but surely, we will collectively begin to realize just how much music is projecting onto us.

Television, another media channel that affects our collective consciousness, has been rapidly evolving since its creation, having gone from black and white to high definition to 3D. Television is unique in that it actually gives us a visual representation of how to manifest our reality. Whether the messages are related to sports, sitcoms, dramas, reality shows, news programs, talk shows, or fantasy, we take these images and use them as examples of how we should feel, act, and relate to one another.

As much as we would like to blame others for the huge influence that TV has on us, we must also take responsibility for our lack of awareness, as we are responsible for the emotions and experiences that we buy into, that are fed to us visually through television. As you continue to expand your awareness, you will start to pick out different conditioning tactics every time you watch television, and you will identify the underlying messages that are being sent to you.

Ironically, the term "program" is not coincidental. When you take a closer look, you start to see just how much these television shows are truly programming humanity.

The first sector of television that has a huge influence on our collective consciousness is sports TV. One of the primary ways that television aids in our conditioning is by instilling a dream to become professional athletes into children's minds. In reality, because of the infrastructure of the professional sports industry, the odds of this dream coming into fruition are slim to none.

Despite these poor statistics, many children latch onto the idea of living the sports dream. This dream creates an external identity that they latch onto, preventing these children from truly revealing who they are.

When we have this picture in our heads of what we think we should be, this dream that is so glamorous, we lose touch with ourselves. Instead of really introspecting and learning about ourselves so that we can cultivate ourselves into the people that we want to become, we keep chasing after this unrealistic dream.

If you've had any past experience playing sports as a kid, I'm sure you've seen how many of your friends that played in either high school or college athletics are still hanging onto those past identities and "glory days." This dream that so many are chasing simply acts as a tool to confuse and lead us away from our personal growth because we start to believe that our best days are forever behind us.

In addition to this, sports also act as a distraction from our everyday reality. There are millions of men worldwide that work their nine to five jobs, and the only thing that they look forward to is a cold beer and a sports game. This keeps us focused on competition, as we build pride for being a fan of a particular team, and we continue to participate in this year-round from sport to sport. This continues to lead us away from our reality and from self-realization, and understanding our true purpose here on Earth.

The next sector of television that we will discuss are sitcoms and drama television shows. These shows leave such a huge impression on us because they have a unique ability to be relatable, allowing us to connect with them on a deeper emotional level. This causes us to create strong emotional connections to these shows. Whether it features a bachelor such as Charlie Sheen in Two and A Half Men, a "broken" family that is relatable to our times in Modern Family, or work-related shows like The Office, we see parallels to our own lives in these shows that makes them so attractive. Most of these shows will provide a few good laughs, but will always leave you with an emotional imprint associated with the message or "lesson" being portrayed.

Drama programs such as CSI or Sex and the City grab your attention and influence you. Whether it's through fear or love, they imprint a message that you will soon manifest into your reality.

In truth, the more a show can grab you and connect with you on an emotional level, the better the ratings and profits will be. We watch these shows because they are entertaining, but as we view these shows with a new level of awareness, we can start to identify the ways in which they are connecting to us on an emotional level and create a distinction between entertainment and internalization.

Lastly, fantasy shows and cartoons are used specifically to engage the human imagination. These shows provide a distraction, an escape from our real life scenarios. Some fantasy shows such as True Blood or The Walking Dead give us an image of an alternative reality that revolves around fear. By spending an hour a day in this reality that is even worse than our reality here on planet earth, we start to develop this idea that life isn't actually so bad within our own reality. This leaves us satisfied and keeps us from questioning the status quo.

In addition, fantasy shows like these also give us the idea that natural disasters and supernatural phenomena are only something that we see on television but will never actually be a reality. In fact, there are many "fantasy" programs that are created based on truth about our universe and our society, but because it is presented as fantasy, we are left even farther removed from understanding truth.

Reality television has taken popular culture by storm over the last 25 or so years. MTV's Real World started off a reality television craze, with six strangers selected to live together, and the viewer is left to see what unfolds.

Today, the reality television genre has expanded into programs about everything from dating shows, to cultural puns, to competitions to discover the next famous person to rise within society. These shows affect our culture by presenting different ways of life for the viewer to latch onto. For example, dating shows teach us how to value others based on an individual's appearance, what they do for a living, and what material items they possess. These shows present ways in which we can approach the opposite sex that are driven by lust and delusion. When we see this we internalize this way of relating to the opposite sex and we recreate it in our own lives, manifesting negative karma.

As an example of how TV perpetuates cultural puns, we will discuss the infinitely popular Jersey Shore. This show documents the culture of Italian ways of life, which are driven through the heavy use of lust and superficial presentation of the self. Though this can be very entertaining, the show is actually creating a way of life for college kids that is inevitably promoting separation.

Lastly, we will discuss shows in the realm of American Idol, in which musicians across the country manifest dreams of becoming the next star. The word fame actually stands for False Admiration Manifesting Ego, which in truth is how most of our stars who acquire fame present themselves.

These shows fuel these dreamers by turning art and expression into a competition that rewards the winner with immediate fame and fortune. There is a tremendous amount of talent and skill in this world, and in truth, all of our artwork is valuable. In essence, by making art a competition, we are reiterating the idea that some human beings are more valuable than other human beings based on the artwork that they produce, when in reality, we are all very unique and cannot compare ourselves or our art or to one another. We need to figure out a way to proliferate and uplift all artists so that they are all helping one another grow, as opposed to pitting artists against one another.

Reality television is just another example of how our society keeps humanity in a confused state of consciousness.

News is another strong and powerful tool of manipulation that drives us into fear-driven states of consciousness. The majority of the information received through the news promotes negative actions that occur within society. The news presents us with live coverage, statistics of increased crime, and what is perceived as factual evidence that we must have caution when it comes to our safety.

Whether it be local, state, or worldwide news, negativity is the number one energy being generated from this form of programming. In order to keep us coming back every day for more news, they mix in a few positive stories here and there, especially stories that have soft messages.

The news informs us about major current events going on at the time, although only disasters are amplified, and when positive events occur on a large scale, they do not tend to be publicized. These newscasts promote the devastation, driving it into our consciousness and our subconscious as great tragedy.

Although many times these stories are indeed tragedies, they tend to be over-emphasized, and they cause us to dwell on different issues as a collective. When we dwell on tragedies, as a collective we start to operate from a place of fear and anger and, therefore, our collective vibration becomes dense.

Many times stories are over-exaggerated in order to causes uproar and disharmony, and stories are also many times created out of thin air in order to create a distraction. For example, when we have school shootings, the news amplifies the feeling of devastation and really hammers this idea of tragedy into our minds.

The news presents to us the emotions of the individuals experiencing this great tragedy over and over, driving fear and pain into each and every one of us. This causes us to live believing that we are not safe, and that we should always be on guard and hold onto those that we hold dear to us. We start to internalize the idea that world peace is impossible to obtain and that our world of separation will always hold dominance.

Talk shows also influence our reality significantly. Popular shows, such as Jerry Springer and Maury, show the rest of the world how "lower" levels of society live. These types of television shows perpetuate the separation between people in different economic classes, reiterating the idea that some human beings are better than others based on the amount of money they have and the lifestyle they live.

When the population watches these shows, they judge these people for the challenges that they are going through and they start to see themselves as more valuable because they aren't in the same situation.

In addition, other types of talk shows such as Dr. Phil discuss many different topics addressing issues within our society and they openly look for solutions. This show in particular appears to be of the best nature, in that it makes an attempt to address specific issues. However, it gives us the idea that there are infinite problems that are present in this world, and that we can't really do anything ourselves to change it. Shows like this make the public feel powerless by presenting so many issues but not really laying out a solution that will target the infrastructure, the root of these issues, so that the fix will be sustainable and long-term.

By reinforcing the idea that we have so many problems in the world, we are actually creating more problems at the same time. These shows bring issues to our awareness, but they do not actually make any changes or provide any solutions.

Dr. Phil does indeed have positive intentions, and we do acknowledge him for that, but we do suggest that he assesses how his work is being executed. It is important to assess exactly what the community needs and what affect it will have before we implement solutions. He may be giving the community something that appears to help them on the surface, but when you take a closer look, you see that what you thought was going to help the community is actually hurting them long-term. This is where Dr. Phil have gone off-course. Once we assess what the community truly needs, we can address the issue from the root, from its infrastructure, rather than treating it on the surface only.

With this new understanding and awareness surrounding television, New Earth Connect challenges you to seek the underlying messages that are intended to influence and condition your consciousness. With this new information we trust that you will begin your process of comprehending the power of television. Television itself is definitely not going anywhere in the near future, but once we are aware of how it is being used to influence us, we can begin to seek ways that we can use its immense power to actually uplift humanity and expand our collective consciousness.

As of today, there are actually a handful of shows that are opening the door to this, such as Ancient Aliens, dramas like Touched, and documentaries that expose truths that have been hidden from the general public.

It's important to tune into your intuition in order to determine what information resonates with you as truthful. Television can either keep us locked in conditioned states or be a huge tool for enlightenment. When it comes down to it, we all have the free will of choice. Therefore, it is up to us individually to recognize and make the appropriate changes in our lives.

The movie industry is a beast of its own because for many, nothing captures a person's emotions like a great movie. Movies impact us massively on a day-to-day basis. Whether a movie is a topic of conversation or we quote lines from movies, film influences our reality significantly, emulating much of the conditioning that takes place within television shows but on a deeper level.

There are endless genres of movies that we could discuss, but we will address the most marketed genres and exemplify what type of energy they are manifesting into our realities. The four major categories are dramas, horror, comedies, and action films.

Drama films usually channel three different energies including love, problem-solving, and overcoming adversity. The energies portrayed in these movies are so powerful because audiences can relate and connect with the stories. This captures viewer's emotions.

The influence that these movies have is enormous because we see ourselves in the characters and the storyline, which makes us much more susceptible to internalizing any messages that the movie may suggest. When we see these movies, we see idealistic and glamorized pictures of what our lives should look like, how we should behave, how we should look to be accepted within society, and much more.

While our emotions are so tightly captured within this relatable story, we cling to these images and strive to conform to these picture perfect representations of people and situations. Because of this, we are not able to reveal our true selves and create ourselves into the individuals who we want to become, but we subconsciously try to recreate what we have seen in films. This prevents us from connecting with ourselves and revealing ourselves.

In addition, when we watch these films with awareness, dramas can also give us insight into how our society's infrastructure of conditioning has developed and evolved over time. For example, movies such as Blow or

American Gangster show us that before technology progressed, the control that the government had over us was not as absolute as it is today.

During the pre-technology era, civilians had more freedom and were able to "get away with much more," so to speak. In the end, however, the government always prevails. When we look at today's society and structure we can see that the control of humanity has indeed progressed. By learning about the history of our system of control, we are able to better comprehend why our society is the way that it is today, and from there we are better equipped to combat it.

Horror films are one of the most marketed genres of movies because they market one of the most powerful and oppressive energies on this planet: fear. Fear manifests low vibrational realities into our consciousness, not only pushing us away from vibrations of love, but actually creating realities of pain and insanity for many.

Movies such as Saw provide very graphic images of torture. By taking in these types of messages on a regular basis, we internalize these low frequencies, which translates into crime, pain and suffering.

Films about the "supernatural" world twist our perceptions of the spiritual realm. For example, some movies may suggest that having faith in your religion is the only way to escape different scenarios such as being possessed or encountering the underworld. Horror movies are a huge negative manipulation tool that get more and more disturbing as the years go on.

In order for us to navigate this powerful negative force, we must collectively cut off our support for this billion dollar industry in order to remove these aspects of our reality from our consciousness. When we stop putting so much energy and attention into this industry, we will allow its influence to slowly but surely fade away.

Comedy films, while providing us with a good laugh, are not necessarily affecting us in a blatantly negative way as horror films are. The way that they affect us is much more subtle, by providing us with a distraction from our everyday lives and from ourselves. These films provide us with jokes and identities to grab onto that we do not create for ourselves, but are created for us.

For example, when the first Anchorman came out kids all over the country were repeating the lines from that movie, some even engulfing themselves completely in the language of the film. Most comedies assist in the creation of stereotypes in society, poking fun at qualities that human beings innately posses. This adds to the separation between individuals within in our society.

Comedies also identify different roles within society, and they label them as more or less valuable than one another. For example, a movie may depict a garbage man's job being less valuable than an individual who is a businessman, when in reality everybody's position in society is equally valuable.

Overall, comedies are not necessarily negative in nature, but they do affect us negatively by influencing us to latch onto an identity that is portrayed to us through these films, keeping us from discovering our true selves.

Action movies create high-level drama with a twist of supernatural powers that citizens can only fantasize about. The primary issue with action movies is that they create fantasy worlds in which people to get lost. There are even massive gatherings, one of which is called ComicCon, where tens of thousands of people attend dressed as characters from these films, spending extravagant amounts of money in the process.

In essence, alternative realities are created that affect the human consciousness such a great deal that many individuals allow these realities to become their lives. These are just another distraction within the illusion of our society that we create that prevents us from expanding and getting in touch with our true nature.

The movie industry produces billions of dollars in profit every year and continues to do its part in the lifelong conditioning process of our global community. With this information we must move forward in awareness, not in fear. It is important to understand that there is much to learn from films if we watch them with a keen eye and consciousness.

In reality, the movie industry is not going anywhere any time soon, but we must make the conscious choice as to what affects us and what does not. Instead of spending our money on horror movies or comedies, we can start supporting films that will help us to expand our consciousness. Our power to change the world begins with the small choices that we make individually on a daily basis. Essentially, it begins with individual change that then will support collective change.

Advertising is a tool of manipulation that all media outlets have in common. A multi-billion dollar industry, these programming tactics aim to convince our minds to spend money. Whether the advertisement is promoting a particular product or service, seeking a donation, or publicizing another program, these forms of manipulation continue to influence our choices and our actions.

Next, we will examine how advertisements are used to grab our attention through topics such as sex, food, alcohol, saving money, law, health, popularity and belief systems.

First and foremost we will discuss how the media uses sex to sell products and services. Since the time that commercials were created, sex has been used to provoke emotions inside of the viewer and manipulate consumers to spend money on a product or service. Sex is a natural human instinct, one that is very intrinsic to our being.

Corporations actually study how they can manipulate a human being's natural instincts optimally to their advantage. When a consumer watches an advertisement that activates this animal-like instinct inside of us, it triggers us to associate our sexual desires with a product or service.

Once this association is created, manipulation becomes very easy, and the consumer will begin to invest in the product or service without even consciously recognizing the connection and how they were lead to make this decision.

Subconsciously we will start to believe that if we use the product or service, we will automatically attract members of the opposite sex or automatically engage in more sexual activity.

These ideals of sex and beauty are placed into our reality in order to fuel our insecurities, making us believe that we need a certain product in order to look and feel better about ourselves. We start to think in line with the classic saying, "if you look good, you'll feel good," and when it comes to these commercials, in order to look good we must use these products that are being sold to us.

As a society, sex is greatly exploited and much of this has to do with how it is used to sell products. Because all of the messages that we see through the media portray sex in a glamorized, exaggerated way in order to sell something, we start to develop this image of sex that is fake. We internalize this picture of what sex should look like, and with this, we create expectations. We're not able to allow sex to be a natural, organic experience for which we are fully present.

When expectations about sex are not met in the moment, we start to be disappointed in the experience. This in essence is oppressive, because sex is an integral part of our beings and our spirits. When the freedom of experiencing sex holistically is taken away from us, it dampens our spirits.

Because money is the driving motivation for our capitalist society, the fear of not having enough money is used throughout advertising to trigger another human instinct that is inside of all of us, that fight or flight response that is based on fear. For instance, car dealers frequently use seasonal savings in their marketing, instilling the idea of urgency into our minds, because "now is the best time to buy a car."

Other marketing tools such as Wal-Mart rollback prices promote grand savings at all times, aiming to manipulate your consciousness to shop at their store exclusively to get the best savings. In reality, we never actually save too much money when you look at the numbers. The majority of stores have similar discounts and deals after marking the prices up and then tricking your mind into believing that there is a huge savings.

In the end, the goal of marketing is to convince the consumer to believe anything that will make the company more money.

Lawsuits have become part of our society's infrastructure and have drastically changed our world by causing us to live in fear of being sued. As a society, because we are motivated by money, we are looking for ways in which we can take advantage of other people's mistakes so that we can sue them and receive benefits.

As human beings, we all make mistakes, and we must help each other grow and move past those mistakes rather than profiting from them. Everywhere we turn, we see advertisements for law firms that we can contact in order to capitalize off of our misfortunes or other people's misfortunes. This unhealthy cycle perpetuates negative karma immensely, and it isn't helping the community as a whole if we continue in this direction.

As we evolve as a society, our population is continuously growing. So much so that within the next 50 years living comfortably in dense areas is going to be an issue. As previously discussed, population control is used to keep humanity from growing too much and getting too "out of hand" for the group of elites that are in control. One huge tactic of population control is the infectious disease that we call cancer.

Cancer has affected just about every single family across the country, and because it is so common, it has created a sense of collective fear across the board. With this sense of fear, many actually manifest the disease into their reality. As a society, we are constantly trying to find the cure for cancer. We are constantly raising money for the cause, and year after year we have been unsuccessful.

Unfortunately, this isn't a coincidence, as there have actually been cures for cancer that have been suppressed by the government. All over the country you see campaigns raising billions of dollars to find a cure, when all of this money is being raised for nothing. As long as population control is in effect, the cure will never be released to us. As members of this society, we can start by raising awareness about the suppression of cures for diseases such as these and move toward rebellion and change together.

As a society we are raised seeking external validation from others as opposed to cultivating value for ourselves. We are not taught how to love ourselves and, therefore, we look outwardly to other people in order for them to tell us and show us that we are valuable.

This is very destructive, because when we are raised in this mindset, our self-love is conditional to others and the way that they feel about us. Essentially, we end up not being in control of the value that we feel for ourselves, and when somebody in our lives such as our significant other leaves us, or we are not accepted by a group of peers at school, our self-worth diminishes. What if we lived in a society in which we all loved ourselves, and did not depend on others to feel valuable?

As children we are introduced to the idea of popularity most commonly in our first years within the school system, when we are beginning to develop our identities. At this very vulnerable stage, and with no knowledge of what it means to cultivate value for ourselves, we automatically begin seeking this validation from our peers. This cycle continues to grow and develop throughout the rest of our lives, seeking validation from our partners, our co-workers, friends, family, and it never stops unless we consciously work toward a different trajectory.

Advertising optimizes this idea that human beings are only valuable based on other people's approval. Different companies use marketing to make consumers believe that if they buy a product or service, that others will approve of them and make them feel valuable. For example, if you wear a certain brand of clothing, your peers at school will accept you, or if you wear a certain cologne the opposite sex will give you validation.

As a society, we need to begin to cultivate value for ourselves so that we know our worth unconditionally, no matter what car we drive, no matter who is in our lives.

Patriarchy and Racism

The infrastructure of The United States was founded and developed through institutionalized patriarchy and racism. This system of hierarchy has largely contributed to the conditioning of our society. This separation of race and sex has created a foundation for us to see our fellow human beings as being more or less valuable than one another based on these inherent qualities. This is the main tool that has brought us to separate ourselves from one another instead of seeing each other as equals.

With a group of Founding Fathers consisting of all white men, our society was built to empower the white male, while oppressing women and other races. From there, a hierarchy was created that puts white men at the top of society and trickles down to men all of others races, to white women, and finally to women of all other races.

In today's society, patriarchy and racism are still very much present, and our generation has been born into a new iteration of its institutionalization. Instead of previous generations that engaged in overt ways of expressing patriarchy and racism, we have been born into an era in which patriarchy and racism still very much exist under the radar. The beliefs and thought patterns that lead us to see each other as separate, or more or less valuable than one another, are still very much present and are deeply ingrained into the way that we think. Many times we don't even realize when these infrastructures influence our thought processes.

All the way back in the 17th century in Europe, women were considered to be the property of men when they were bonded in marriage. This is where the tradition of the women taking the man's last name derived from. Continuing forward in our history, in the years of 1850 - 1900, men had the ability to send their wives to mental institutions without their consent for "illnesses" that were questionable. Women were diagnosed as insane because of religious excitement, epilepsy, and suppressed menstruation.

The labeling of women as insane was frequent and done without question, and this has largely influenced society's perspective toward women. This is why today you so commonly hear men referring to women as "bitches" or being "crazy" when they speak up and express themselves. When a man expresses himself outwardly, nobody ever calls him insane.

In the 1700s when slaves were freed, and then proceeding throughout our history when black people were given equal rights, there was an external fix, a Band-Aid so to speak, that was placed onto the issue of racism. While the laws were fixed externally, the way that people perceived and felt about black people did not change. The deep, internal hatred was not resolved or unpacked. Therefore, black slaves were "freed" into a society that set them up to fail, a society that had a deep hatred for them, that had previously looked at them as nothing more than objects, property there to serve.

The same has remained true for women. On the books, women now have equal rights, but internally, the way that men perceive women has not changed. Very deep down, men still see woman as being there to serve them, to cook and clean for them and to be beautiful trophies that they can show off to their friends. Simultaneously, women have internalized this belief about themselves and actually believe that they are less than men.

This is what is called internalized patriarchy. Once a population has been oppressed for such a long time, they begin to believe that whatever they are being told about themselves is true. After a while they don't have to be told anymore because they are telling themselves. This gets passed down from generation to generation, through parents who pass the mentality down and through what society teaches as a whole. The same internalization goes for the black population.

There is racism that is still very present under the radar, and we are actually in denial about it. It is very possible that many people who will read this want to reject these ideas immediately. This is because we don't want to believe that we are racist or sexist, because this makes us "bad people."

Throughout our lives, all we have been taught is that it is bad to be racist and sexist on an external level. In truth, we are more afraid of other's thinking we are racist, rather than being concerned about why it is actually wrong to be racist.

When we take down this barrier of being scared to be perceived as racist or as bad people, we can really begin to look inside of ourselves and see how the infrastructure really affects us on a day-to-day basis, through our daily thought processes. For example, a white man or woman may walk down the street and see a black man and automatically put his or her guard up, while when passing a white man he or she may not think twice about it. This white person isn't a bad person because he or she intentionally decided to be racist. These thoughts allude to classic conditioning.

This thought process is a product of our upbringing. It is portrayed to us in all forms, through the media, through our parents, through our peers, etc. Bringing attention to this reality allows us to really unpack it and start to break down those barriers that separate us from one another.

By bringing this awareness to our thought processes, we are able to identify these thoughts, where they are coming from, and have a discussion with ourselves about it. Once we ask ourselves questions, we are able to really see how these thoughts don't make sense. We did not choose these thoughts, they were chosen for us.

It often seems that the police, along with the rest of our population, have racism deeply ingrained into the way they think. We do not question this automated way of thinking, and that has led in many cases to the deaths of innocent black people. The police, like many others, in these cases did not question their automatic profiling. This led them to take action that was based on this error in thought, error in judgment that took people's lives.

These are just amplified examples of the errors in thought that each and every one of us makes every single day. It could be as small as meeting a black person and not listening to what he or she has to say as intently as you would a white man.

These are things that we can easily deny to ourselves if we are not being honest. Instead of getting angry at the police, let's see how we are actually mirrors of them, in small, everyday situations like this. Let's make the appropriate efforts to unpack this inside of ourselves first and, from there, we can be the change that we want to see in this world, as opposed to pointing fingers. When this occurs we can spread this outwardly by setting the example and teaching others.

Love

Love is an energy that everybody within our society is searching for. Most don't truly understand it, but everybody is striving to find it and experience it.

As our society sees it today, love is a deep feeling of affection toward another human being. It's something that you can fall into and out of, and it's something that you are obligated to give to family members.

These are the most defined and recognizable conceptualizations of love that our society holds true. Love then, in essence, is conditional to another person, and we will no longer feel this love when this external source isn't there anymore.

On a universal scale, however, love is something much greater.

Love stands for "Living One Vibrational Energy" and is a universal frequency that can be accessed by all human beings at all times. This frequency represents the 5th dimension, or what many may call the heavens.

Our society uses the strength of love to separate us and trick us into believing that love is something that is found outside of ourselves, or in another person. In truth, when we as individuals learn to love ourselves, we will naturally draw true love to us.

The majority of us live our lives continuously searching for something that already exists inside of us, we just have to access it. From the time we are born we are taught to love and seek love from exterior things.

Love is empowering and, without it, the society that we live in would not continue to exist. This is the only way that we know how to access the frequency of love. Because of this, we continue to feed this desire for love every day by searching for exterior sources.

As a collective, each and every individual must go through his own process of cultivating love for himself and, from there, we will begin to see a shift in our overall collective consciousness.

As previously discussed, throughout the media and within popular culture we see images of who and what society says we should be, and we latch onto these images. Because of this, we never actually discover our true selves because we are striving to match those images. Something that we must understand is that the body is temporary and the soul is infinite.

All of the exterior labels that we place on ourselves, whether it be our level of popularity, our roles within society, who we associate with, or how much money we make, directly contributes to the illusion of confusion. With this, society separates itself into groups of people who are better or worse than one another.

As a universal spirit, we have made the conscious choice to incarnate onto this planet. Everything that we experience in this life is intentional, and we choose to experience these challenges in order for our souls to learn and grow. No matter how tragic the challenges that we go through may seem, we must remember that our spirit has chosen these experiences. Confusion and pain work to distract us from truly learning from these challenges and accomplishing our life purpose here on this planet. Because of this, we must consciously identify these life images that we subconsciously try to replicate and move toward a life that we create for ourselves.

The first step in revealing our true selves is letting go of the image of ourselves that we have created throughout our lives up until this point of awakening. This will most certainly be a challenge, as we have developed thought patterns and habits that translate into comfort zones that we do not want to leave. We get very stuck in these comfort zones and because of this, we get very resistant to change.

In addition, we are also taught to hold onto the past and use it as an excuse for our current patterns of action. In essence, we use our past to stay in a place of victimization rather than using our awareness to move forward and create something more productive for ourselves. For example, we might say "I am this way because my parents were alcoholics or because I was in trouble with the law." We choose to stay a victim of our situation and we choose to believe that we can't change.

We can either choose reiterate patterns of behavior that do not serve us or we can choose to create new trajectories for ourselves. We must stop feeding those negative patterns and making excuses for our actions. We cannot collectively influence the world positively unless we work on ourselves first and foremost. In order to reveal our true selves we must first let go of our past selves and be open to change and revelation.

True love comes from an understanding of who you are and, with this, you can use New Earth Connect's Code to Your Soul system to discover which energy your soul chose to incarnate.

Once you can grasp how the numbers work in conjunction with your emotions and experiences, you will have much greater control over what you create. By gaining an understanding that there is a male and female energy connected with a particular Zodiac, chakra, and element, you can begin to draw connections to the specific energy that resonates with you the most.

When you begin to use this system strategically, your relationship with yourself starts to flourish because you are finally getting to know yourself. Once you begin the process of introspection, you slowly but surely will put the pieces of the puzzle together and reveal yourself for who you truly are on a soul level.

Part II:
The Code to Your Soul for The Body

The elements, chakras, and Zodiacs are what make up the characteristics of our body and, yes, they do incorporate traits that effect our mind, but they mainly work with our bodies persona.

The **elements** are the key to our personal rhythm as they affect the way we flow through our daily lives and interactions. (For example, Air signs are more often than not very quick-witted individuals.)

The **chakras** show us what part of the body our energy stems from, while also acting as a physical energetic system that, when balanced, can provide long-lasting health and beauty. (For example, Virgos are the throat chakra and, when stressed, they can develop sore throats or neck pain.)

The **Zodiacs** are our physical appeal and ego. They govern the way in which our persona perceives the world and others. Understanding what it means to be your inherit Zodiac will help you better navigate your world socially. (For example, Aries are The Ram and rams have great horns. More often than not, Aries tend to be very focused on their hair, a.k.a horns.)

When you are able to combine the characteristics of your element, chakra, and Zodiac you will feel much more balanced in yourself and your emotions.

Wondering how this all works together? Well, here's an example...

If someone is a Sagittarius, that means that they're a fire sign and are in the third eye chakra. This tells us that this person needs to properly stimulate themselves (Fire). Since the third eye chakra is in the forehead and its meditative focus is illusion, it would behoove this Sagittarius to stimulate themselves with genuine experiences. When they lie to themselves or others, they can create illusion in their reality, leaving them with a mega-headache and clouded vision when looking towards future goals.

So let's take a closer look at each of the elements, chakras and Zodiac signs to gain a better understanding of their unique needs and traits.

Elements

Elements are a huge component of each individual's energetic makeup. Each Zodiac is aligned with one of the four elements. There are both masculine and feminine elements; air and fire are masculine, and water and earth are feminine.

As we go into detail about the four elements, we will explain how they work in conjunction with one another. By gaining an understanding of what your element is, how it works, and what it does, you can begin to create balance inside of yourself.

You may have noticed that we have presented the elements from most to least dense. Air is everywhere at once. You can't see it, but you can feel it. Earth is hard, and you can walk on it. Water is also very hard once it is frozen. Fire you cannot touch, and air you cannot even see.

Air

The Zodiacs that are aligned with air are Aquarius, Gemini and Libra. Air is a masculine element that is very deeply connected with the heavens.

You can see the effects of air interacting with the environment. For example, you can see how it blows the branches on a tree, but you cannot see the air itself.

Individuals who possess air as their element have a naturally mystic personality and are very deep thinkers. These individuals are also very swift physically and mentally, as air has the ability to move quickly. Because of this, it is important for air signs to avoid interacting with stimulus that slows them down and distracts them.

In addition, air signs must always be aware of their breath. Some air signs suffer from asthma because they tend to rush through their thoughts, emotions, and expressions. Because of this, when it's time to deliver what they've been cooking up, they begin to hyperventilate. Meditation is very important for air signs, as the ability to calm the whirling winds in their heads can bring them great success. Meditation allows them to stay calm, centered and grounded while developing their great ideas and life purposes.

When it comes to working with other signs, air can work successfully with all signs, but this versatility can backfire on them.

We will start by explaining the dynamic between two air signs working together. All air signs are very intelligent and have a great ability to read behavior. When you put two of these signs together, the relationship resembles two psychologists working together. This has the potential to be a very successful pair if both parties are comfortable with constructive criticism. Because they are both air signs, they are able to pick out insecurities in other people quite easily. This can either develop into a long-lasting relationship in which both parties are constantly helping each other grow, or it also has the potential to fizzle out because one of the two air signs can't handle the high-intellect dynamic of the relationship.

One of the most exciting pairs for the air sign is a relationship with a fire element. When air comes into contact with fire, it stimulates it. A fire sign will love working with an air sign, as they are both masculine elements and will enjoy the strong, fast, and competitive lifestyle. But this can also backfire.

Air signs are very smart and witty, and fire signs want to be in control and always be right. If the clever air sign begins to notice any slip-ups in the fire sign, she will be quick to point this out. If the fire sign does not like being held accountable, he may get annoyed and the relationship may come to end. Because of this, in a relationship with a fire sign, the air sign should discover channels to positively stimulate herself while continuing to incorporate new things into the relationship. In essence, keeping the winds blowing will keep the fire alive.

When air works with water is it important for air to be sensitive to water's pace. Water and air are opposite signs, as water is feminine and air is masculine. When you see water flowing peacefully in a backwoods stream, this is a sign that the two elements are working in harmony with one another. When you see a hurricane, it is apparent that the two are not working well.

Making sure that they are in tune with their partners' pace can be tough for most air signs, considering they love to fly around in any direction and at any speed. The water sign must find the sufficient flow.

As an air sign, having the ability to push or pull at the flow of the water at any moment, it is important that they do not create hurricanes. This dynamic is similar to the relationship between air and fire. However, a water sign will have a tougher time fighting with air because the water sign will usually either freeze up her emotions or leave the relationship.

The last element that air can work with is earth. Earth is the slowest and most dense of the four elements, so if air is interested in earth, it is important for earth to obtain a certain level of confidence and security. If an air element that moves without being seen is willing to slow itself down to connect with an earth sign, you know that there must be a really special connection.

Earth is a feminine element, but air and earth are opposites in other ways as well. Earth possesses a much calmer energy than air and, therefore, many air signs are drawn toward earth's ability to calm the mind and be present, a practice of mindfulness.

This relationship has the potential to be a wonderful experience for both signs. But if the earth sign is unable to harbor confidence in the ability to stay present, the air sign will more than likely fly away to something else that is stimulating.

This versatility means air has "the pick of the litter." Air has a personality that makes him able to fly around and hang with all three elements, but an air sign will only find true harmony when at a pace that is comfortable for him.

Fire

The Zodiacs that are aligned with fire are Sagittarius, Leo, and Aries. Fire is also a masculine element. Fire signs are strong physically and mentally, as fire has the ability to overcome all obstacles. This ability to dominate many aspects of life must be approached with a humble attitude. Fire signs must understand and remain aware that their energy is very strong, because they have the tendency to intimidate others with this strength.

It is essential to look at how fire signs treat themselves. The knowledge that they are capable of anything can lead them to be very hard on themselves when they come up short. Their fire burns bright, but if they constantly put themselves down, they will put out their own flames.

If they are too hard on themselves and put out their own fires, they can become lazy and unwilling to attempt anything in life. This laziness will lead them to beat themselves up even more and create a nasty downward spiral.

Because of this, it is very important for fire signs to be easy on themselves and the people around them. In other words, they should use their fire to ignite the task at hand, not burn it to ashes.

In regard to relationships, we will begin with fire on fire because we have already touched on fire with air in the Air section.

When fire works with fire, it can be a most exciting relationship filled with adventure and passion. These two can stimulate each other, and the fire will burn so brightly that people will recognize their energy from miles away.

These two signs also have the potential to bump heads quite frequently. Fire signs enjoy being the leader in a relationship. Because of this, two fire signs together will fight for the lead, which can bring about disagreements due to the competitive nature of the relationship. If these two signs are together it is important for each of them to enjoy his own fire and the fire that his partner possesses. They must both realize that no one is better than the other, and each individual has an equally bright flame.

Fire and water it is the classic opposites attract relationship. Some individuals truly enjoy being with an opposite match, while others do not. The fire sign could very much like moving at the pace of the water sign, and water signs tend to have their own unique mystical ways of living that can attract the fire sign. Fire signs appreciate intellect, and water signs carry a large amount of intellect.

The issue here, however, is that the fire sign can move too fast and burn too brightly for the water sign, leaving it dried up, a cloud of mist. In addition, the water sign can be so set in her own pace that she actually puts out the fire. It is important in these types of relationships to make sure that neither element pushes the other. This way, each can survive alongside the other.

To discuss how fire behaves with earth, we must take a moment to think about what fire does to the earth in the realms of Mother Nature. If you let fire burn for too long, it will scorch the earth. This is exactly what happens within this relationship.

If the earth sign is unable to harness the fire and keep it at bay, the fire will completely dominate the earth. In some circumstances, an individual in a relationship will enjoy being dominated by his partner. The majority of the time, for earth signs to enjoy being with fire, the two must agree on the balance of power. If they do, the relationship can be very enjoyable, because after all, earth has many wide open plains on which the fire can run; the fire just needs to be conscious of how hot he burns.

Water

Water is aligned with Pisces, Cancer, and Scorpio and is our first feminine element. Water signs are full of knowledge and unique creativity. Water signs must discover the pace or flow that works for them. Water has the ability to rip down rivers like rapids or it can lie in a lake of tranquility. Either way, the water sign must discover the way in which she likes to move. Once that discovery has been made, the water sign will find the confidence to show all of her unique abilities.

Trial and error is a huge part of finding that flow, so she must not be afraid to try, fail, and then try again. Not only do they discover their true flows this way, but they also gain vital information for their journeys through life.

Because we have touched on water with air and water with fire in the previous sections, we will begin by discussing water with water. This can be one of the more harmonious relationships. Because this relationship has a dynamic of two feminine energies working together, there tend to be immense amounts of love and passion between two water signs.

This relationship is made or broken depending upon their ability to flow together. If one water sign wants to be a rushing rapid and the other wants to be a smooth, slow stream, there will usually be an issue. These two signs must come to an agreement about the speed of their flow.

In addition, because both of these signs are very intelligent and unique, they must be careful not to coach one another too heavily. It is important to allow one another to move in their own unique ways, while maintaining a balanced flow with one another. This is the most difficult part of bringing these two signs together. This will allow each to be his or herself but at the same time link their flows harmoniously with one another.

Earth and water can also engage in a very enjoyable relationship together. Similar to the dynamic between two water elements, both of these elements are feminine and, because of this, when united, these signs can harbor very passionate love. The earth harbors oceans, rivers, lakes, and streams. Just as the earth is home to water in so many forms, when these two signs come together, their energy works well together, as earth will welcome water into his space warmly. But if the water sign, tries to manipulate the earth, the relationship won't go very well.

If you observe nature, you will notice that when a wave crashes into a rock the rock does not budge. Because of this dynamic, it is natural for the earth sign to take command in the relationship. The earth sign doesn't take command to control the water sign, but because the earth sign has the potential to put the water sign in a great position for success. This is why this relationship is so exciting.

When the two are working in conjunction with one another, their talents both shine. In essence, the water sign will be able to show its uniqueness, and the earth sign will be able to show its strength.

Earth

Earth is another feminine element, and it is aligned with Taurus, Virgo, and Capricorn. Earth signs tend to be the most tranquil and steady of the four. They enjoy the process of many things, and they love sprouting roots to grow. Hence the many beautiful forests and gardens that our earth has to show us.

The key to success for earth signs is just that. They must find their preferred soil and let their gardens grow. Many earth signs have trouble finding their true passion, so they jump from soil to soil never taking the time to grow solid roots.

Once they find their passions and decide where they want to be, the ability to create a solid foundation is almost effortless. Once the foundation is set, they are able to extend their roots, and a beautiful garden begins to grow.

We have already discussed how earth works with the other three elements, so we will now discuss earth in a relationship with earth. This relationship can be strong and beautiful, but only when both earth parties are grounded. Earth signs can be undisciplined, so if one of the signs has already set up solid roots and the other is still unsure of where he wants to be, the relationship is doomed. If they are both able to agree on a certain soil, these two together can blossom the most beautiful gardens.

Chakras

There are seven chakras or energy centers in the human energetic body that go from root to crown. Each of them carries its own unique characteristics, but they all must work harmoniously for an individual to be balanced. Chakras look like beautiful lotus flowers in all different colors. They spin clockwise when they are balanced and clear and counterclockwise when blocked and unbalanced.

When individuals get stressed or are struggling in different areas of their lives, certain chakras in their bodies can close up, leading to a blockage in energy flow. The Zodiacs are aligned with certain chakras, so the energy of the chakra will be predominant in the Zodiac that is aligned with it. In the upcoming passages we will introduce the chakras and the Zodiacs and characteristics that align with them.

The first chakra we will discuss is the **root chakra,** which aligns with Capricorn and shows in the color red. The energy is located in the area from a person's legs to her toes.

The root chakra is the most dense chakra of the seven. It grounds us and gives us stability. Each chakra has a meditative focus, and fear is the focus for the root chakra.

To clear the root chakra, there are different exercises and techniques that we can use, and we can also set intentions of letting go of these emotions. In addition, when working to clear the root chakra, we can work on navigating our fear through introspection, asking ourselves where that fear originates from, why we're feeling it, and how we can heal it.

The second chakra is the **sacral (or sex) chakra**. The Zodiacs that align with this chakra are Cancer and Scorpio, and the color is orange. The energy is located within the sex organs, right below the belly button.

The sex chakra is a very creative chakra because after all, our sex organs are the vessels for recreation. Because of this, harboring a confident level of creation is key for those working to open up their sex chakras.

The meditative focus for this chakra is forgiveness. It is very important for those trying to open up this chakra to forgive the people around them, but most of all, forgive themselves. Sometimes these people can feel that they overexerted their creative energies, and they will beat themselves up because of this, so forgiveness of the self is vital for their happiness.

The third chakra is the **stomach chakra**. The Zodiacs that align with this chakra are Aries and Leo, and the color is yellow. The energy is located in the stomach.

The stomach chakra is very powerful because if you think about the human body, many vital organs are located in the stomach area, organs that we need to live. These organs are very powerful because they break down food, filter toxins out of our bodies, and much more.

The meditative focus for this chakra is shame, so it is important for us as a collective to not be ashamed of our power. It may be difficult at first to use their powerful energies, but once they're confident in how to deliver their power with no shame, they will find great happiness.

The fourth chakra is the **heart chakra**, which aligns with Taurus and Libra and is the color green (or pink for the high heart, which is "invisible," and everyone who is trying to open the heart chakra must believe that it is there).

This energy is located in the heart, in the middle of the chest. Blockages here can occur largely through past relationships, current relationships, and our relationships with ourselves. The meditative focus, grief, aligns perfectly with understanding how to properly open up the heart chakra.

The five stages of grief are DABDA (denial, anger, bargaining, depression, and acceptance), and we can work with each of these stages to navigate a blocked heart chakra, especially acceptance. It is important to understand and accept that the things that we lose are only gone temporarily and are never gone forever. When this acceptance occurs, stress will be relieved and the individual will be able to move on to the next adventure.

The fifth chakra is the **throat chakra**. The Zodiacs that align with this chakra are Gemini and Virgo, and the color is blue.

The energy is located in the throat, and once again, if you think about the human body, our throat is where we get our voice from, where we express sound. Therefore, it is important for individuals attempting to open up this chakra to express themselves truthfully.

The meditative focus for this chakra is lies. Many times theses individuals will talk themselves into trouble and, because of this, they lie their way out of it. They can even lie to themselves and become delusional. It is important that they stay honest with the people around them and most importantly with themselves.

The sixth chakra is the **third eye chakra**, aligned with Sagittarius and Pisces, and colored indigo. This energy center is located in the center of the forehead.

It is said that the "third eye" in our heads is actually looking directly up into the heavens. It is our medium of communication with the heavens, and individuals who are working this chakra are highly intuitive.

The meditative focus for this chakra is illusion. Because this chakra is very intuitive, these individuals have the mental ability to trick and deceive. It is important that they use their high level of intuitiveness for good, so karma doesn't bite them back with some illusion of its own.

The last chakra is the **crown chakra**. The Zodiac aligned with this chakra is Aquarius, and the color is violet. The energy is located outside of the body and above the head, hence the name crown chakra.

Because this chakra is not attached to the body, it is important that individuals working with this chakra are careful not to over-attach their energy to dense energies, and that they also don't detach themselves from this dimension. In other words, they must find a happy medium between connecting with the spiritual plane and staying grounded. If they are unable to balance the two, they will most likely carry great stress.

The meditative focus for this chakra is let go, which is perfectly aligned with what they need to do. It is important for them to let go of the fact that they are different, or "not attached," and maintain interaction with the rest of us. Once they are able to let go of all criticisms, they will find great happiness.

When it comes to relationships and pairing the chakras, we've found that each of them work quite well with one another. We've seen same-chakra relationships be very harmonious, but we've also seen them rub each other the wrong way. We've also seen complete opposite chakra relationships be harmonious but in other circumstances clash greatly.

The key for understanding relationships with the chakras is understanding that the lower chakras (red, orange, yellow) are more dense, and that the higher chakras (blue, indigo, violet) are less dense.

The heart chakra is the bridge between these spectrums. If you are a lower chakra and have had trouble with people who were higher chakras, maybe it's time to look for a lower chakra, and vise versa.

We have noticed one small grouping within the chakras.

If you look at the root, the third eye, and the crown, you will see that there are only four Zodiacs aligned with them, and all four elements are in that group as well. Capricorn brings the earth element, Sagittarius brings fire, Pisces brings water, and Aquarius brings air.

If you look at the other four chakras, sex, stomach, heart, and throat, you will notice that there are eight Zodiacs and each element is there twice. The sex chakra is water/water, the stomach chakra is fire/fire, and the heart and throat chakras both carry earth, air, earth, and air.

When closely examined, it seems that there is a small grouping that fits inside the seven chakras.

This does not rule out the possibility of a root chakra liking a heart chakra, but it does mean that there are some cosmic groupings that go along with these energy fields. We suggest that you experiment as much as you can on your own and discover what energy attracts you.

The Almighty I Am Statement

"I Am" is one of the most powerful statements in the universe because whatever words you utter after it will manifest into reality.

When you declare anything with the words "I Am," you are putting energy into the universe and affirming that it is true. Because time is just a unit of measure, all realities exist at the same time, in the "now moment." Because of this, when you declare with the "I Am" statement in that now moment you become that.

The trick is to continue to instill this confidence inside of yourself, and a great way to do this is using "I Am" statements in your meditation, prayers, while you are talking to yourself, or in diary entries.

However you communicate with yourself, use the "I Am" statement. Provided below are "I Am" statements that align with each chakra.

Root: I Am Grounded, I Am a Survivor, I Am Secure, I Am Abundant

Sex: I Am Creative, I Am Intimate, I Am Sexual, I Am Balanced

Stomach: I Am Powerful, I Am Energized, I Am Centered, I Am Whole

Heart: I Am Loved, I Am Compassionate, I Am Emotionally Balanced

Throat: I Am Communicative, I Am Expressive, I Am Healthy

Third Eye: I Am Open, I Am Seeing Clearly, I Am Intuitive

Crown: I Am Connected, I Am Understanding, I Am Aware, I Am One

These statements align with some of the emotional issues of the chakras and Zodiacs, so if you are having trouble balancing a chakra, affirm the "I Am" statements that go along with it.

In addition, once you are in tune with your most dominant chakra, it will also be beneficial to use these affirmations to balance the other chakras as well, while harmonizing your energy systems and developing the ability to connect with others more efficiently.

Zodiac

In addition to elements and chakras, we are each affected by the Zodiac.

Here are the dates traditionally ascribed to each of the signs.

Sign	From	To
Aquarius	January 21	February 19
Pisces	February 20	March 20
Aries	March 21	April 20
Taurus	April 21	May 21
Gemini	May 22	June 21
Cancer	June 22	July 22
Leo	July 23	August 22
Virgo	August 23	September 22
Libra	September 23	October 23
Scorpio	October 24	November 21
Sagittarius	November 22	December 21
Capricorn	December 22	January 20

However, we've found that the traits displayed by people born until each sign is affected by the individual's gender as well. So while the male and female of a sign share certain characteristics, there are distinct differences as well.

Aquarius Man

The Aquarius man is quite interesting. He is very smart and very appealing to many people, but he is often very detached, and it is difficult to hold his attention. As an air sign, this man moves from experience to experience gaining knowledge along the way while sharing any information that he can with others.

When he feels comfortable enough to stop and really enjoy the experience that he is in, he is a joy to be around. Getting this very detached man to settle down and enjoy the moment is key. For the Aquarius man, balance is extremely important.

If he isn't detached he can many times be the opposite, very attached, fearful of letting go and seeing what new experiences lie ahead. For him to have any fun and success in this world he must slow down and connect to the experiences he has been provided with. In addition, it is also important for him to always remember to let go and move on because there are many great things that lie ahead.

In his youth the Aquarius man acquires a multitude of interests, as he many times tries different sports and different hobbies, meeting new friends and sometimes even changing schools once or twice. All of these different experiences allow him to gather information about where he truly wants to focus his energy. He can also lose the opportunity to continue to learn because he is many times unable to let go of what he has recently found. If he is unable to let go he will eventually become very irritated because he longs to discover new information.

When he is stuck in the same place for a long period of time, he is not able to gather new information and experiences. When he is able to let go and move on from experience to experience he finds that his world has so much to offer him.

As he grows older and discovers what he really wants, he is able to find success through the group of people that he decides to trust. Deep down inside he knows that a team of intelligent minds is always better than one working on the same project, but trust is very difficult for the Aquarius man to harness. This is usually because his trust has been broken in his youth because he has trusted too easily. When he develops trust inside of himself, he is then able to trust others. When this occurs the sky is truly the limit for him.

These same concepts apply to the Aquarius man when it comes to love. As he is naturally detached, it is common for him to be wary of trusting others. He often treats love as just another experience to try out and then quickly leave.

As he grows older he realizes how many times he has pushed true love away, and as a result he can become clingy. It is important for him to find this balance between committing and moving onto something else. He must also know himself well enough to realize when he has found his perfect match.

The Aquarius man is so good at attracting partners because of his vast intelligence and, because of this, he doesn't see what is directly in front of him. When this occurs, it is important for him to slow down and take notice of what he is currently experiencing.

The Aquarius man is hard to chase but good to catch, so it is important for him to realize this about himself. He must carry the confidence that great things always lie ahead of him, but he must also be humble enough to treat each and every experience like it will be his last. When he carries himself with a humble and confident grace he will be adored by all and find success in whatever he puts his energy into.

Aquarius Woman

The Aquarius woman is one of the more caring women within the Zodiac. She possesses a fun and lovable energy that many really enjoy being around. As air signs these women are very smart, and they are also great teachers. They long to be accepted by everybody and because of this, they rarely put up any resistance. This can many times lead them to situations in which their friends and family walk all over them.

When they gain the confidence inside of themselves to trust what the universe provides, they will discover that in every moment there is something amazing for them to see. When they can develop trust in the universe this will allow them to properly apply their wonderful intellect and care to those around them.

When looking for love it is important for the Aquarius woman to always know that true love is available. They must believe in this true love and, from there, they are able to seek the right energetic match.

As an air sign, she wants to connect strongly with her physical world. In her head she thinks a million miles a minute, and in her heart she feels the emotions of others very strongly.

With all of this energy flowing through her, it can be difficult for her to settle down at a young age. She becomes hyperactive because she knows what she wants to do and say but has a lot of trouble expressing and executing. When she feels embarrassed by the way she expresses herself it leads her to feel a great deal of anxiety.

She has a great deal of natural beauty and, because of this, she can be lead into relationships that stroke her ego because most individuals aren't afraid to tell her how beautiful she is. Because of this, it is difficult for her to see who truly loves her for who she is with her excited and upbeat personality, and who is only around her because she is beautiful and is recognized as a sociable woman.

When she gains a better understanding of how she can most efficiently deliver her beautiful energy she will find herself in more situations that are safe and in which she is able to trust. Harboring the ability to properly apply her immense caregiving energy will open up many doors for the Aquarius woman.

She will find that her goals in life are easily achieved when she trusts that the universe will provide for her. She has so much care and information to pass onto others that doors will fly open for her, because the people who open the doors are eager to hear her wisdom. This will instill a great deal of confidence in the Aquarius woman, which will allow her to continue helping others and gain more knowledge about how to go about it.

When it comes to the arena of love, this woman tends to get caught up in the theatrics of life. All of the drama that surrounds a relationship will weigh heavily on the shoulders of the Aquarius woman, so essentially, it is very important for her to steer clear. When she has confidence in herself she will come to realize that anybody that treats her poorly isn't worth her time or energy. With this realization she will be able to find the perfect partner that will compliment her radiant energy. When she finally chooses the right one they will be happy and healthy as long as they stay focused and committed to one another.

The Aquarius woman will very much enjoy her time here on Earth if she is able to relax into who she is and what she has to offer. When she tries to do too much and be someone other than herself she will get hung up with anxiety and self-doubt. Her ability to relax into life and into herself will help her to access her confidence. This confidence will allow her to flow with the energies of life very gracefully, becoming a beacon of joy for all to see.

Pisces Man

The Pisces man is one of the most intelligent and capable men in the Zodiac. Being a water sign he is very wise and has the ability to move at his own flow quite easily. This can be a problem for the Pisces man, because he can be too caught up in the idea that no one else is on the same page as him. This can make him very bitter toward the rest of the world, which can lead him to shutting off from communities and isolating himself.

It is very important for him to understand that some people may in fact not be on the same page as him, but that does not give him the right to judge them. He is actually slowing his own personal momentum down by complaining about things that are out of his control, and judging others instead of helping them come to his understanding.

When he is able to accept everyone for his or her own pace, he can properly lead by example. This ability to lead by example will instill a great deal of confidence inside of him. When he is confident in himself he has a much greater level of patience for the rest of the world.

While growing up the Pisces man can be very difficult to deal with. He is very intelligent at a young age, but has not refined his delivery of his knowledge. Many individuals may perceive what he has to say as being impolite. This can lead him to "getting in trouble," or getting reprimanded by authority figures around him.

This can have a couple different effects on the young Pisces man. He will either become more agitated and rude when he tries to make a point, or, because he is fearful of coming off as rude, he will fall into a spell of low confidence that will make him very shy and unwilling to share his knowledge.

The young Pisces man will look for external validation, or another source outside of himself that will help him to feel confident. This external validation many times comes through the form of hobbies such as sports or music, or he may find a romantic partner just to show his peers that he is desirable.

This search for confidence outside of himself will lead him nowhere. He may experience great success in whatever he chooses for a certain period of time, but the success will not be sustainable. Human beings can only count on themselves and, therefore, if they rely on an external source, what happens when that source is no longer there?

It is important for him to take a step back, regroup, and create confidence from inside of himself. He must realize that, yes, he is capable of being the best player on the team or the lead singer in a band. When he understands that he is all of those things because they all come from within, he will finally be at peace. Not only will he be at peace, but he will also flourish in whatever he sets his mind to. When he begins to flourish he will see that he has no limitations.

When it comes to love, it is important for him to have a great deal of self-confidence. He must also be humbled by whomever decides to walk next to him. The Pisces man can certainly be a handful, as all of his strength and intelligence can be overwhelming. Because of this, when he is over-confident he can come off as brash and rude.

When he has low confidence he is usually led to be with the wrong person. When he finds his right match he must focus carefully on the balance of give and take between his love life and whatever other goals he has set for himself. He doesn't want to lose the love of his life just because he couldn't get out of the office and spend time with his partner. When he creates balance in his life the right romance will find him.

The Pisces man can do it all, but he must be humble and merciful to his peers. When he learns how to carry himself with a lovable grace, positive attention is a guarantee. This positive attention will compliment his own energy and will radiate positively to those around him. With this new energy he is able to continue on his journey of success. He must always remember that his confidence is only a positive contribution to those around him when he is sweet and humble.

Pisces Woman

The Pisces woman is smart, strong, and very beautiful. When she is young it can be very hard for her to balance her high velocity energy, so she can be prone to fits of anxiety and frustration. Through that anxiety and frustration she will look outside herself for confidence and love, and this can lead her to having poor experiences with her peers.

She can be seen as an outcast for quite some time or, when she blossoms into her true beauty, she can be used by the men she attracts. All of this negative attention adds to her insecurities, so it is important for her to see her beauty and her value and, from there, she can develop herself into the person that she wants to become.

She has to get to know herself and understand what makes her tick before she can share that with anybody else. Coming to this understanding of herself will help her find her perfect partner.

When she is young she has too much energy for her parents to handle. In the school setting her personality and her jaw-dropping eyes can make her popular amongst her peers, but she is known to engage with the drama because all of the attention that she is getting can backfire if she is not secure with herself.

Her journey to creating self-security comes from finding expression. She usually believes that the most effective way to express is to be popular amongst her peers, but in truth, the best way to express is to discover the voice that lies inside of herself.

When she begins to discover her true expression, no matter what that is, the attention that she attracts will be much more genuine. She has a sharp intuition, and as she harbors her own expression she will have a better ability to gauge who is genuine in her life.

As she grows older and discovers herself and her expression, she becomes a force to be reckoned with. She can accomplish any goal that she sets her mind to. Now, if insecurities are still present inside of the fish lady, she becomes very harsh and very difficult to deal with.

It is important for her to understand that mentally she is one step ahead of the game and, because of this, it is wise for her to practice being humble and showing a great deal of care while working with others. When she's working by herself she can be as hard on herself as she'd like. When she is working with others, however, it is very important to tap into her empathy and mother-like qualities while also being patient with others.

When it comes to finding the right partner, she will only attract them into her life when she finds love inside of herself first. Pisces women are so beautiful that in many instances they attract people into their lives that only love them for their beauty.

When she discovers herself in her life and her experiences love will come into her life. This love will be somebody who wants to fly upwards with her and, together, they will help each other grow and expand, rather than keeping her where she is and admiring her. This match that flows with her will allow her feel true love, rather than mere admiration. When she finds this perfect partner, their potential together is limitless.

For the Pisces woman, the world is in her control when she believes in herself and really cultivates this control. If she continuously looks outside of herself for the answers and for confidence she will be very upset to discover that the search will be never-ending. Love that is cultivated from within will open every door that she comes into contact with, and this will bring her a huge amount of confidence and harmony within her life.

Aries Man

The Aries Man is strong, passionate and confident, but sometimes those qualities can make him come off as too macho and detached from his feelings. As a fire sign, these men tend to be very aggressive throughout their lives. Aries men want to be the best, and more often than not they view themselves as the best.

The physical appearance of the Aries man radiates masculine energy, whether he has a more boyish look, or a burly man look. No matter what side of the masculine scale the Aries man falls on, he is always sure to keep himself very clean cut. The ram is the Aries' animal sign, and just like the ram, Aries men like to take care of their horns.

Growing up the Aries man can develop a particularly misogynistic outlook on life due to their relationships with their parents. This outlook can lead Aries men toward finding a partner that they can "rescue," so that they feel they have the power in the relationship.

It is important for the Aries man to remain secure in his confidence. When the Aries man becomes insecure, he can be very cold-hearted, but when he embraces his true power with humble grace, he is loved and admired by all.

When thinking of an Aries man it can be helpful to imagine two things. The first is a great big ram staring you down ready to charge. The second is the element of fire, burning brightly and passionately. Aries men are just that, they are constantly full of energy and ambition, which can quickly turn into rage and aggression if agitated.

The Aries man is very confident and assured of himself, as he feels that he knows exactly how to approach life. Whether it be working in the stock market or making it as an unsigned musician, the Aries man is confident in his abilities to be successful in any area of life.

Aries is a fire sign and that is exactly what drives the Aries man. That fire burning in his belly keeps him moving forward past his obstacles. Because Aries men are so confident, they rarely bond with other men. They usually see other men as either competition or just small helpers along their divine paths to greatness.

All of that confidence inside of the Aries man is usually due to the fact that on the outside he truly is the apple of everyone's eye. The Aries man embodies the classic masculine physical appearance.

Interestingly, the scale of appearance for them is very wide. Some Aries men have an extremely boyish appeal, with soft pale skin and tiny physiques, and other Aries men are big brute men, standing well over six feet tall with hairy chests and backs.

No matter if the Aries man is all the way on one side or somewhere in the middle of the spectrum, he emanates masculinity. Just as the ram has beautiful horns and a strong chest, torso, and legs, so does the Aries man.

The Aries man is very focused on his appearance. Most specifically, he almost always maintains his hair. Whether he has a trimmed beard, gives his hair an edge, or grows it all out and rocks the long hair, the Aries man is constantly focused on how he looks.

When the Aries man is young he is more often than not brought up by an overbearing mother and a detached father. This is where all of the insecurities in the Aries man develop. Because his mom is overbearing and gives him so much attention and his dad barely around, the Aries man will usually try to prove himself as much as possible. Because of this, you'll often find him in playground fights and attracted to women who won't even dream of voicing their opinions.

The Aries' mom has given him a bad taste for strong and confident women, so he'll usually look for a woman who worships him and won't try to direct his life. When or if he finds that woman, the dynamic of their relationship will usually lead the Aries man to become distant from her just as his father was to his mother. The Aries man will find women to act as his playthings until he has his "love at first sight" moment.

In addition, he also wants to set himself up for this grand, amazing, theatrical moment of meeting the woman of his dreams. This is because he wants to feel as if he chose her, and this allows him to feel in control.

Aries men have all of the qualities to be dominant and successful. It is important for them to allow themselves to be balanced in their egos by being confident but not allowing it to become competitive and aggressive. It is important for them to allow their looks to be charming but not to invite resentment from others. When an Aries man can see strong women as another bright mind that can help him, rather than a nagging opinion that is trying to change him, he will succeed. If he is able to embody his internal fire without burning others with it, there is no limit for the Aries man.

Aries Woman

The Aries woman is confident, competitive, and goal-oriented. Aries is a fire sign, so strength and aggression contribute to the way that Aries women dominate their worlds. The Aries woman is very strong and competitive, and because of this she tends to enjoy working alone rather than with a team. If she is going to hang out with a group, it usually consists of all men.

The Aries woman usually retains a youthful complexion throughout her whole life. Like the ram, an Aries woman has a very strong and athletic body, which breeds even more confidence. This confidence translates directly into her love life, as the lady ram likes to be in control, and she'll move on to the next without considering any hurt feelings.

By observing her parents she develops the mindset of not wanting to be trapped by a man, so many times she will seek a partner who she perceives herself to be "better than" and, therefore, she believes she will be able to leave the relationship more easily.

If you're looking for an Aries woman, look for a large group of men, because this ram lady isn't like the other ladies of the astrological block. She is the quintessential tomboy and, therefore, she won't be found in the kitchen making Thanksgiving dinner because she's most likely out back playing football with the boys.

An Aries woman also has a strong sense of confidence, which leads her to enjoy working alone. She is a powerhouse and doesn't want to be distracted in any way. Because of this, she rarely goes out of her way to assist others. To her, most women are too "girly" and are usually uninteresting to her.

She fights to be seen as an equal to men, and attempts to compete with them. Here, we can see how the patriarchy in our society has influenced her to reject her own sex and attempt to be seen as an equal to men.

She will not embrace other women nor her own feminine qualities. If an Aries woman is unaware of how this conditioning from society is affecting her, she will continue to fight to be the alpha and, whether her opponent is male or female, she wants to win.

The Aries woman executes her life plan with ease and grace. She attracts all sorts of men who she most commonly uses to her liking and then moves along to find another. She doesn't usually lean toward the idea of settling down too soon because she is much more focused on achieving her individual goals. Because of this, sex becomes a tool to her, a means by which she can get a release.

Her strong and athletic frame allows her to do two things quite well: play sports and dominate the bedroom. Both activities are something the ram woman finds enjoyable.

In their youths, Aries women are more often than not exposed to a pushover mom and an unemotional dad. This contributes to her perspective that women are weak and unimportant and, therefore, she is drawn to emulate her father. She seeks out weaker men that she can dominate so she can make sure that she is not treated how her mother was treated.

This behavior goes hand-in-hand with her already unemotional approach to relationships. She's always more focused on her own achievements than caring for another in a "serious" relationship. This cycle of behavior will continue until she finds that one type of guy that fits her exact needs. He has to be a manly man like her father, but at the same time he definitely cannot push her around. This will allow her to continue to feel as if she is in control, while also feeling accepted by the guys because this man fits into the category of "a man's man."

Like the ram in full sprint, there is no stopping this woman when she gets a head of steam, but like most rams, she can be quite hard-headed.

It is important for Aries women to feel confident when embracing their natural feminine sides. They are already so strong, as it is in their nature to be. By embracing and opening up to the more emotional side of their beings, they will feel more balanced and therefore become even more successful.

Aries woman, enjoy the fact that you can hang with the fellas while most women don't. The fire burns brightly within Aries women, but they shouldn't push it outwardly and burn those that are just there to admire the flame.

Taurus Man

The Taurus man is patient and powerful like the bull that represents this sign. Being an earth sign, his passive approach to life allows him to carefully pick and choose his endeavors. Although he may appear as just another good-looking, quiet guy with nothing to say, on the inside he is filled with passion and creativity that is waiting to be unleashed.

Like the bull, Taurus men are built strongly with elegant grace. Their build is a metaphor for their personality, as they are very tough and have a strong core, but have soft skin and a youthful complexion.

He usually tends to grow up under a dominant mother and a passive father, and this leads the Taurus man to get closer to his mother. With that being said, the Taurus guy's mother can become over-dominant in his life, leading him to look for women who will worship him in order to compensate. When the Taurus man is confident in his beliefs and carries himself with a strong sense of self-worth, the sky's the limit for him.

The Taurus man greatly resembles his earth element. Just as the earth slowly and methodically changes from season to season, the Taurus man truly embraces the slow and steady approach to life. He rarely jumps out of his shoes to grab something right away. Even if it's something he particularly likes, he'll still wait to observe the situation before making a move. This approach can lead people to view the Taurus man as too laid back and carefree. He can sometimes come across as lethargic, but that is just the way he functions. He is never afraid of having a good time, but he is careful to choose what he's going to do.

Because he is very particular with his likes and dislikes, he tends to run with a crew that very much enjoys exactly what he enjoys. Many times the Taurus man wants to be the unchallenged leader of the gang. When challenged by another, he can be quick to give up and say, "Okay. The gang is yours, I'll go do my own thing," while proceeding to find another gang of like-minded people.

Built like bulls, these men are usually strong with solid cores and very defined features like the face of a bull. Just how a big, beautiful bull can catch the eyes of many in the room, Taurus men are aware that their appearances can have the same affect on people, so they use it well in the many arenas of life.

They are most commonly fast and coordinated, built great for contact sports like hockey and football, but most Taurus men enjoy leisure sports like golf so they can play and socialize, using their natural charm to move up the ladders in whatever field they choose.

Their natural charm has a way with the romantic side too, as Tauruses tend to attract many people, but sometimes it's not for love, just attention and confidence boosting. Fear of rejection is huge for the Taurus man, so to prevent serious heartbreak they rarely dive too deep into the waters of love. As they get older and gain a greater sense of who they are and what they want, they do tend to finally settle down.

At a young age the Taurus man usually has a highly involved mother and a detached father. Because of this, the Taurus can be conditioned to see women as dominant threats and men as just friends to relax and hang with. The high involvement from his mother can lead him to feel pressure from her, leading him to seek praise from women. His search for praise from women can get him stuck in the mindset of finding women who will worship him, because he longs to be able to have control in a relationship since his mother was always micromanaging him.

The detached experience that he gets from his dad can influence Taurus men to be laid back and nonchalant, as they grow up seeing very little fire and strength from their fathers. Because of this dynamic from their fathers they are commonly too cautious and fearful of rejection.

The Taurus man is capable of many things when he is comfortable in his choices and beliefs. His cautious approach is great for him when he has balance within. He must allow himself to be selective, but at the same time, he must be confident in order to take chances because he is full of ability. If he is too shy to show people his charm, no one will ever know how great he truly is.

The relationship with his parents is just another way to show him that passion and expression are both integral parts of life, and they need to be balanced. When he is balanced he will no longer feel the need to get praise from women, so his ability to find a solid significant other is enhanced.

When his mind is balanced he will attract other balanced, like-minded people, and the Taurus man will get what he always wanted, happiness surrounded by people who share his interests.

Taurus Woman

The Taurus woman, an earth sign, is one of the most feminine signs in the Zodiac. She is more often than not dripping with natural beauty, but the bull lady also likes to indulge materialistically, so you can usually catch her decked out in makeup and jewelry.

She is very big on helping others and usually finds a career in which she can do so. She is sometimes involved in too many things at once and because of this she may not take care of herself. Taurus women have a strong belief that money is power, and as a result, they will often put money in front of their own happiness. Whether it be a man with money or a job they don't particularly like, they will engage in it only to get what they want out of it. At the end of the day the Taurus woman is a helpless romantic and isn't going to settle until she finds her perfect match.

To find a Taurus woman, all one needs to do is use their senses, listen for the jingling of bracelets, smell for the sweet scent of perfume, and look for those big beautiful bull eyes, batting their long eye lashes right at you. That's her, exerting all of her abilities in order to attract your attention. Many bull ladies are fascinated with the little tricks that they can use to attract others into their lives. Most of them are so naturally beautiful that they could walk around naked and wouldn't ever catch a bad look, but to them, if something is beautiful why not dress it up in even more beautiful attire?

This is a double-edged sword for the Taurus lady, as she gives herself a lot of confidence when she dolls herself up. At the same time, however, she attracts a lot of attention, especially from men. Now just like a bull, the Taurus' sight is rather shaky, so with all that male attention it can be hard for her to see which men are good for her. A slew of bad relationships can be a part of the young bull's life, but once she realizes how powerful her beauty truly is, she has much better control over who she lets in.

As an earth sign, a Taurus woman usually takes on mother earth-like qualities. She loves to help, whether she becomes a school teacher, a doctor, or someone who owns a health food store, she is always trying to help others better themselves.

Tauruses, like bulls, have tons of energy and are real go-getters. As a result, they are usually working on large amounts of projects. This creates another double-edged sword that they must navigate. It's wonderful that they want to help others, but in order to help others she must help herself first. A lot of the time Taurus women get so caught up in their many projects that they forget to take time for themselves.

When they have a solid foundation inside of themselves, they are much better fit to be successful in their projects. They can forget that they naturally draw to themselves whatever they desire. For example, money won't come to them until they are comfortable in their environment and they stop trying to pull it out of the universe and just allow it to flow to them naturally.

Something important for all Tauruses to remember, especially the women, is to have patience. An important teaching for these women is not to push circumstances in life, but to let everything fall into place. This is parallel to how a bull might be most successful. If a bull is running toward you, you'll certainly run away, but if it is sitting calmly, you'll be very intrigued to go right up to it.

Growing up, Taurus women tend to have a strong, over-disciplined mothers and soft, relaxed fathers. This leads the Taurus woman to resent her mother for ruining her father's passion for life. This aggressive nature of her mother is what leads the bull lady to embrace her girly side. She wants power and respect, but she is unaware that she can receive that by just being herself. She uses her mother as an example of what she should not be.

The Taurus woman realizes that her beauty allows her strength and power to pour out of her, and she knows she doesn't need to be a tyrant. When she is involved in an energy that is all power-based and not based out of love, she will be quick to get out of it in order to find her power through love. When off-balance, she can be lured in by rich men, but no matter how long it takes she will eventually realize that she is all that she needs, and money and power will come to her when she is balanced.

Her beauty and her brain will inevitably cause her success, not another being. She can sometimes be duped into opening herself up for others, but once she finds her own self-worth, she has much better control of who she lets in. When self-worth is flowing smoothly through her body, she is able to find great success in whatever she puts her energy into.

Her Mother Earth qualities make her a great companion for whomever she chooses to grow old with. It is important to note that if she chooses you and you aren't able to meet all of her needs, she will find someone else. The bull lady won't stop until she gets her perfect match.

Gemini Man

The Gemini man is a classic air sign. He is very much in his own head, but he is a deep thinker and a fun person to be around. He is great at attracting a slew of friends to set out on an adventure with, as people generally view him as the person who shows everybody a good time. This can be a good thing or a bad thing for the Gemini man, as he always has great ideas and is a fun person to be around, but all of that energy can lead him to rarely completing a task. He is the guy that never stops, which makes his mind jump from idea to idea. Many individuals perceive this as the Gemini man having multiple personalities.

He is not necessarily always society's idea of "handsome," but that does not mean that he is not inherently beautiful. He has a silver tongue and can talk his way into or out of any situation, business or romantic. It is important for the Gemini man to find a way to channel all of his energy while discovering confidence in those outlets. Gemini men often find themselves in negative environments or situations because they need a place to focus their powerful energy. When they find productive ways to release their energy, the perfect high-energy person will gracefully run his or her way into the Gemini man's life.

To find the Gemini man look for the guy who is surrounded by laughter. The twins fellow always brings the life of the party, and those

around him are all well aware of that. He is a joy to be aroun
always getting into an interesting new hobby that others are willing to join, and many will even enjoy just observing him at work.

Just as his mind moves quickly so does his body. Gemini men are built with speed and strength and are usually very talented in sports. If they are not able to discipline themselves, however, they won't ever go anywhere with their immense abilities. Gemini men can be successful in the arenas that they choose if they remain focused

Too many times the Gemini man loses confidence in the early stages of a task, gives up, and goes on to repeat this process with another task. If he is able to navigate a lack of confidence, his potential is limitless.

The twins guy has a smile that is infectious and inviting, which is why he has no problem finding confidence in social settings. His smile and charm give him the ability to captivate anyone that he talks to. The Gemini man, however, can sometimes get easily excited and talk too much, leaving him feeling like he has shown his cards too soon. The key for these men is to know that people are already interested in what they have to say, and there is no need to oversell themselves.

The same thing applies when Gemini men work with the opposite sex, as women already find them fun and interesting, and because of that, the more they stay confident in their fun and fast-paced style, the more they will want to join in on the fun.

When the Gemini man is young he can be exposed to a set of parents who have no time for him because of their own challenges. His mother can be very strict, and his father is usually involved in his own world. As a result, the Gemini guy is pulled between the two and usually takes his mother's side because she is around more frequently. This causes him to distrust men in the future, and he always watches even his closest friends very carefully. This can also lead him to cycle through friendships and relationships throughout his entire life.

Because his energy moves quickly, if he no longer trusts someone, he is never afraid to keep it moving and find another partner. It is very important for the Gemini man to trust himself. Once he believes in his own words and actions, he will be able to see more clearly.

With an everlasting energy he is quick to blind himself in a cloud of dust if he shuffles his feet. If he believes in his direction, he can move as fast as he wants to without blinding his vision. When he is confident in his direction he will be able to link up with another energy that is moving at the same rate as he is. When he finally meets his running mate, he will feel at ease with his trust issues because he will feel he has met an equal energy to his own. Gemini men should be confident and focused in their beliefs and they will catch those dreams that they are chasing.

Gemini Woman

The Gemini woman is very strong and capable, but as a fast moving and even faster thinking air sign, she sometimes trips herself up. With a big and exciting energy, she is always surrounded by friends, but they usually tend to be a group of males. The Gemini woman isn't very interested in the cute, fluffy and girly side of life, as she would much rather kick it with the fellas. This side of her allows her to climb up the social ladder with ease.

Although they prefer to hang with the fellas, they most certainly possess a great amount of feminine beauty. They are able to use their looks to get things that they want, although this can sometimes lead them into situations that don't benefit them in the long run. Finding ways to control their high-paced minds and use their strength for good will help them find success in life.

When she is in balance she will naturally attract her mate, as she is very strong and smart. It can be difficult for men to handle her, but when she's balanced, he'll want to be with her because he knows that he can handle what he sees. With her father usually not being around and her mother busy with her own problems, the Gemini woman is left to grow up on her own, which is a huge part of learning how to control her wild energy in her early years.

When the Gemini woman's confidence is lacking she can get distracted and find herself all over the place. She enjoys exerting her dominance, which can be difficult for other women to engage with. She has a very strong will no matter what she is fixated on at the moment.

This high level of energy is a gift and a curse for her. It allows her to be viewed as an attractive partner for a business venture or a romantic relationship. If she is not able to control her high energy, however, she may eventually spin herself up in her own whirlwind, leaving her right back at square one trying to use her energy to attract somebody.

She is very smart and very talented, but the lack of attention from her parents at a young age has made her overly-aggressive when displaying her skills. The confidence to calmly and gracefully go about life is something that she must harness before she can experience true success.

In her youth it is hard for her to find a trustworthy mate. She goes in and out of her emotions, which is usually caused by her lack of parental attention. On top of the emotions that are running high, Gemini women naturally attract men. No matter what size or shape she is, she has all the features that a man wants in a woman. Because of this, most of the time when she is hanging out with men at least a couple of them are interested in her romantically. This can lead her into many situations in which her trust for men might be lost.

She is much more comfortable hanging out with men, and men also enjoy her company. This attention that she gets from men makes her the envy of all of her friends, as she has a natural ability to get along with the guys. The guys think she's cool and the other girls just wonder how she's able to remain confident while engaging in all of the typically male-oriented activities that they enjoy. She is only able to do this when she is confident in who she is and what she enjoys.

This confidence usually does not manifest over night, as during her early teenage years she usually tends to be less confident. With parents who don't really pay her any attention, she is forced to go through the early stages of young adulthood on her own. Frustrated with her youth, she tends to want to grow up as soon as possible. This usually causes the other kids to perceive her as being annoying or too aggressive.

This desire to grow up quickly can leave her in a tight spot when she has grown up. She spends so little time expressing herself in her youth that when she's finally an adult she is tired and beat down from lack of relaxation and enjoyment. In addition, her ability to express herself has diminished, and she is left feeling bitter about her life. To prevent this, she must find healthy ways to express herself. Whether it be with a mate or by herself, she must always express herself. Blocked expression for Gemini women can bring out their unconfident and aggressive sides.

A huge part of her experience here on Earth is to balance her business life with aspects of her life that give her pleasure. Geminis are the twins, and these women are known to sway back and forth between the two. This is a lifelong challenge for the twins lady. If she can enjoy her strong personality but at the same time love the expressive side of herself, she will be able to avoid swaying back forth between the two sides.

Gemini lady, take a deep breath and believe in yourself because after all, you basically raised yourself and you have all of the ability and potential in the world. Find that balance and happiness will find you.

Cancer Man

The Cancer man is one of the more artistic men in the rainbow of Zodiacs. He is smart, usually very clean cut and is also very aware of his appearance. Even when he's not blessed with the "greatest looks" in society's eyes, the Cancer man is always aware of how to make himself very presentable.

As a water sign he is highly intuitive and deeply in touch with his feelings. Cancer men feel much more comfortable with the opposite sex. This usually stems from growing up in a household with only females around. Even if this is not the case, the crab guy has a natural ability to link his energy with any and every woman.

Just like a crab, the Cancer man has a hard exterior with a soft interior. Expression is key for this guy. If he is unable to express himself in productive ways, he can continue to spin his wheels throughout his whole life. Trying to find a female counterpart to help him stimulate this expression is big for this guy. He tends to search for a woman who will serve him, but this won't help stimulate his enormous expression.

To find a Cancer guy, look for the one guy within a group of girls. There is just something about this fella's energy that allows him to link up with women effortlessly. At a young age the crab guy is accustomed to the high emotional energy of women that he develops into a motherly energy for those around him.

Spending his early years trying to help everyone around him, the Cancer guy can end up building a wall to separate himself from his own feelings. Too focused on fitting in with the guys in his class, he ends up blocking his emotional creativity. Not until he relaxes and embraces his true self will he finally be able to unleash all of that expression and creativity that is locked deep inside of the crab guy's shell. Like the moon that rules this sign, the Cancer guy has two sides. You'll see the shy side first, and then eventually the expressive side emerges.

Because he is so aware of his appearance, he knows exactly how to hide himself. With overgrown hair and plain clothes he will make sure he's just another face in the crowd. This is because he is fearful of coming out of his shell. He will only talk to a few people and rarely will cause a big commotion because he isn't very confident in himself.

The other side of him is the expressive side. The crab guy is bursting out of his shell to show all of the artistic ways he is able to express his beautiful soul. Usually buried for years, when this guy finally lets out his expressive side there is no turning back and definitely no ignoring him. Once he is confident in his ability to express, he can affect the emotional state of any room for the better.

Once the crab guy is out of his shell and enjoying himself to the fullest, he begins his search for the perfect match. These guys are natural romantics; they are able to attract many different types of women once they open themselves up. The girls will flock to this hopeless romantic, but he is very picky as to which girl will be his princess.

Because he spent most of his youth trying to help others with their problems, he usually starts with a few girls that will cater to his every need. Our crab guy, however, has a problem with being lazy, as he tends to be challenged in really manifesting anything productive with his creativity.

Because of this, the key for the crab guy in having a successful life and a successful relationship is to find a woman who will aid in stimulating his massive amount of creativity and expression. With that woman by his side he will feel secure and empowered, as those two feelings are key for our crab guy to step up to life's plate and knock a fastball out of the park.

The Cancer man must embrace his deep emotional side, because when that side is opened up he is whole. He will always be strong on the outside, for that crab shell is hard to puncture, but once he believes in his appearance, his words, and his creativity, he will find that life and the people in it are very intrigued by him. Success will come rushing into him like water flowing through a broken dam if he is comfortable in allowing it to come to him.

If he is unable to enjoy the softer side of his crab self, he will never find true success in what he puts his efforts into. Unlocking that soft side will not only help him climb the career ladder, but it will also draw the right woman to him. A woman that will aid in stimulating the best, most creative emotional parts of the Cancer man will be the partner that will help him reveal the best in himself.

Cancer Woman

The Cancer woman is an emotional freight train. Just like the crab that represents her Zodiac, she is hard on the outside and soft on the inside. Do not be fooled, as both sides are heavy on the emotion and passion.

Because she is a water sign, it is important for her to allow her emotions to flow through her rather than for her to try to resist them.

Because of her heightened emotions, many perceive her as the classic damsel in distress, but that is not the case. It is very important for the Cancer lady to take action and be confident in the emotions she is displaying. Only when she is confidently in control of her emotions will she be able to find success in life.

She grows up in a household in which she is more often than not forced to carry out a slew of chores while her mother gets walked all over by her father. The Cancer woman gets the wrong idea of how women should be treated by men. When she is able to confidently assert herself, her Prince Charming will come into her life and treat her how she deserves to be treated.

To find a Cancer woman you need not look far, as you can simply look for the first woman that catches your eye. These women exert so much emotion from their being that it is hard to refrain from taking an extra glance at them.

Sometimes it may even appear that this woman is on the verge of tears, but that is just this water sign's natural state. She is so full of overflowing emotions that anyone in close proximity can be affected. This great amount of emotion causes heavy emotional swings in the crab lady, and it is bad news for anyone that is in her path when she is upset.

She can complain a great deal and will always have someone to complain to because she naturally draws company and attention to herself. When she doesn't want this attention she is quite skilled in disguising herself. Just as quickly as she can grab your attention with just one look, she can disappear from the crowd easily. If this crab doesn't want to come out of her shell, she most certainly will not.

For the Cancer woman to find joy or success in life she must find a way to navigate her emotions productively. At first this process is challenging for the crab lady because in her attempts to navigate her emotions she can come off as aggressive or frustrated, thus attracting unwanted attention.

When she is able to have confidence in how much emotion she lets out in each interaction, she will gracefully glide her way through life. Like water flowing effortlessly down a stream, this woman is in control of her direction while at the same time cascading around the obstacles in life with ease and grace. Because a Cancer woman is a natural artist, people want to see her express herself, but she will only be able to do so when she feels confident in herself.

When insecure with themselves they will do anything to attract approval from others in order to help fight the fear of loneliness. This can many times lead them to get trapped in relationships. They must find the self-confidence to be on their own and fulfill themselves without relationships. When they find that courage to be on their own, they are able to discover how to work their unique set of emotions.

When working their energy and emotions correctly they are able to attract a harmonious relationship that is very worthwhile. This relationship will be a continuous exchange of confidence, which is very important for the Cancer woman. When she feels that the energy exchange is equal she will happily come out of her shell and show all her expressive talents.

The Cancer woman must believe in herself, navigate her emotions productively and find the strength when she is by herself. She has so much expressive energy to offer the world, and it will only come out in the right way when she trusts herself.

These women should focus on how much they enjoy the flow of life, while also finding others who flow at the same pace. It is important to avoid individuals who block their flow, as they are not worth their time no matter how it may seem. When balanced, the Cancer woman's energy is contagious and because of this, they will always find new people and new adventures.

Leo Man

The Leo man, like the lion that represents this sign, is a proud leader. From birth to death he carries himself with a strong confidence. As a fire sign, he is always filled with energy and is very eager to be productive and accomplish tasks.

This high energy can act as a double-edged sword for the Leo guy throughout his youth. He has grown up competing with his siblings for praise from his parents, and this can lead the Leo to be either overly confident, or on the other hand, he can lack confidence and reject competition out of shame. This is an ongoing problem for the Leo throughout his life. He must find a way to use all of his strength and energy in positive ways or he will develop insecurities about himself throughout his life.

This ongoing battle with expressing his abilities also translates into his relationships. Rarely does he ever let anyone get close enough to see all that he is able to express. It won't be until he is ready and he finds a relationship worthy of his time that he will finally let loose and expose all of the beauty locked up inside of this great lion.

You'll know a Leo when you see a Leo, as he's usually the man that looks like he just finished chopping down a tree or running for three touchdowns. They're "manly" looking men in society's traditional sense. These lions tend to take care of their manes whether they have long hair or short, and they're usually dressed very well and are very professional.

Like the lion, they can be lazy and full of themselves and, because of this, it is very important for the Leo man to stay humble. They're very smart human beings. If the Leo man gets lazy or arrogant, he is very quick to realize it and hold himself accountable. If he lacks self-confidence, he will fall deeply into a hole of shame and low self-worth.

It is very important for them to focus on having positive interactions with everyone around them. The more that they see how others believe in them, the more they will be able to cultivate this confidence in themselves. It is important to remain humble, as he will only receive support from others with humbleness.

The lion, however, has a tough time being humble because in his youth he was always competing for approval from his parents. In most circumstances his mother was always supportive of him, but his dad was most likely either not around or was tough to impress. Because of this, the young lion has a difficult time coping with the lack of recognition from his dad. As a result, he will usually lash out in ways that can affect him negatively. One way that he does this is by being overly confident in order to get his dad's attention. If he still doesn't receive his dad's attention he will most commonly lose confidence in his abilities. With this loss he either continues to perform poorly or he will give up completely.

This entire cycle can be prevented if he is able to relax and can give love and approval to himself. When he gains comfort in the work that he does he will find it much easier to be humble.

When the Leo man is comfortable with what he brings to the table, he is better fit to find a match. Family is big for the Leo man, but he is careful in who he selects to help bring his lion cubs into this world. Usually he won't settle down until he feels his career and professional life are where he wants them to be.

If he is off-balance and is in a relationship, it is usually because he is not getting the appropriate attention that he needs from the relationship. This can lead to messy breakups and added stress for both parties. It is important that the Leo man does not give away his energy and power to just anybody because it will lead to resentment.

For the Leo man, life can be a breeze if he is confident himself. When he is confident, his actions will be admired by many, allowing him to receive the praise that the king of the jungle deserves. Once he has comfortably settled into his purpose in life and is accepting of praise, he is able to share his energy in a positive way. This energy is very special and when he is able to express it the right way the possibilities in life are limitless.

Leo Woman

The lioness of the Zodiac is a wonderful, fun loving, ball of energy that everyone enjoys interacting with. As a fire sign, she is built with great passion and charisma, but she will only be successful when she is comfortable controlling all of this energy.

Like the lion who represents her sign, she is a natural hunter and seeks out what she wants and attacks it with power and precision. Growing up in a household in which her parents are most likely absent from her life or are just too busy to give her any attention, she is forced to traverse life on her own. This causes her to discover life in the most difficult ways many times.

Once the Leo lady understands how to properly work her powerful energy, she is a force to be reckoned with. She generally goes for a relationship that contributes to her high energy but never allows that relationship to distract her from her goals in life.

Leo women are easy to find because more often than not they are the girl in the group with the most powerful energy. Whether it is her voice that carries across the room or her flashy clothing and jewelry, she always stands out.

This characteristic acts as a double-edged sword for the lion lady, as she loves and craves attention, but when she does not feel comfortable with who she is, she can begin to feel depressed about how she carries herself and the attention that comes with it. Only when she learns to control her explosive energy will she no longer feel shame for her uniqueness. When she is in control she has a powerful energy and intellect that allows her to tackle any task that she sets her mind to.

In her youth she is usually brought up with a set of parents who are either too busy to give her attention or that ignore her because they are overwhelmed by her massive energy. This leaves her to figure out life on her own, which can be a difficult task in her teenage years. She'll go from high to low self-esteem. Sometimes she can even go from being very popular to doing something that ruins her reputation.

All of this is just a learning process for the Leo woman to figure out just how powerful her energy is and how to properly display it. When she is able to display her energy with control she naturally draws people to her, thus giving her the attention that she longs for.

When it comes to engaging in relationships, it is important for her to be in control of her energy. Many times she is too much for her partner, and she can actually scare them off throughout the early stages. When she has control of her energy she can begin to embark on a relationship.

She usually looks for a match who has high-energy and substantial goals. She enjoys linking her highly passionate energy with somebody else who also has high energy because she knows that together they can be unstoppable. This forward-striding relationship is appealing to a Leo woman because she does not like to be slowed down or get stuck within a routine. She won't settle for somebody who will be complacent. The Leo woman wants to move through tasks quickly and traverse goal after goal. Because of this, she wants to find a partner who is also goal-oriented and fast-moving.

With so much passionate energy, this woman is a real catch, but only when she is confident and comfortable in her great energy. This confidence comes from years of trial and error in navigating challenges. Once she is in control of her great energy this world is just another easy chase and catch for the lion. She can complete any task that she sets her mind to, and she will find a partner who has the ability do the same. When she does, and they both attack life with the same passion and energy, they're a force to be reckoned with.

Virgo Man

The Virgo man is an earth sign and is a very interesting fellow. He is very smart and very aware of the world and how things should be, but that also makes him very critical of himself and his surroundings.

With this built-in criticism, he is quick to have issues trusting those around him and he is also very cautious. He is so careful and cautious that he can sometimes miss out on great opportunities, thus leading him to feel that he's never going to catch his big break to unleash his highly creative side.

The same thing applies when he is involved in a relationship, as he can be over-critical or over-cautious, leading him to miss out on something great. He usually craves instant gratification or immediate results or answers to help him overcome his suspicions in relation to his endeavors. He is prone to rushing into situations and not displaying patience in allowing these endeavors to unfold.

Patience is key for the Virgo man, as he must understand that life is a wonderful journey and that he can cultivate peace of mind if he stops judging and just enjoys it.

A Virgo man stands out easily because he always shows his emotions on his face. The Virgo man is either greeting you with a big excited smile or a clearly depressed face. No matter which one they greet you with, it'll be hard to change once he has made a choice to be in a certain emotional state.

The Virgo man is very set in his ways and is very in-tune with his intuition. The trouble with this is that it can be challenging for him to control his emotional state. The emotional highs and lows are a product of the Virgo guy not knowing exactly who he is and where he truly fits in on the emotional ladder.

More often than not, the Virgo man is all wrapped up in the business side of life, therefore, he is most concerned with accomplishing tasks. When he is too focused on accomplishing tasks he can become suspicious of his life and those involved in it. In addition, he might also begin to feel as if nobody else cares about his endeavors like he does. This will leave him to lose momentum on the task at hand, which can eventually lead to the project falling apart.

To avoid this type of outcome it is important for him to open up to his creative side. This will allow him to find some creative joy when attempting life's tasks. When he is able to find creativity, he naturally relaxes into life, trusting the journey that he is on. When the Virgo man is relaxed and is in a trusting mindset, he is a joy to be around and is a great asset for any group or team.

When it comes to relationships, creativity can really contribute to a thriving companionship for the Virgo man. It is pertinent that he remains light and calm with his partner for many reasons. When he is relaxed and calm, his intelligence is not intimidating to his partner and will be perceived as light and playful.

For the Virgo man, relationships spin slowly and consistently like the Earth on its axis. The more deeply he allows the relationship to develop, the more enjoyment he will render from the partnership. When he tries to rush or force something out of the relationship, it is likely to spin out of control.

A great future lies ahead for every Virgo man once he believes in who he is and allows life to exist without heavily criticizing it. When he sits back in a trusting mindset, he can easily accomplish his many goals and he is a wonderful friend and teammate.

Keeping both his creative side and business side well-fed but also in control will give him great power over his life. He will be able to navigate through life with ease and grace on his way to finding his perfect match. Once he finds somebody who enjoys moving at the same pace as him, he will have enough self-worth to know that he or she is there to stay.

Self-worth is key for the Virgo man, as a person with low self-worth tends to make irrational decisions. The Virgo man should avoid pushing the panic button and remember that he has the tools to handle the situation.

Virgo Woman

The Virgo woman is an earth sign and is an amazing lady. She is beautiful, smart, and if she is working her energy in a productive way she is quite the entertainer. Expression is the key for this woman, and it is important for her to focus on caring for herself.

Throughout her life she is constantly in a battle between not caring for herself and then caring for herself. This inconsistency leads her into situations in which she finds it difficult to trust, and this contributes to her lack of self-worth.

When her self-worth is low she becomes a doormat to those who cross her path throughout her life. Whether it might be friendships or romantic relationships, she must stay confident in her looks and personality. She has been blessed with both, but they are only perceivable to others when she sees them in herself.

The Virgo woman is built with curves and soft innocent eyes. Outshining her beauty is always her personality. She has a laugh that carries across the room and draws everybody's attention. The key for Virgo women is to relax into themselves, allowing their amazing personalities to come through and shine.

Many times she is very aware that she is pleasing to look at and, because of this, instead of embracing her beautiful eyes and telling a joke, she gets caught up in the fact that people are looking at her and she gets nervous.

Virgo women are also very critical and, because of this, she will beat herself up for getting nervous. This leads her to encounter many experiences in which she will allow her self-worth to diminish.

When she takes a breath, slows down for a minute, and gathers herself, she harnesses the energy of the earth. The Virgo woman becomes very powerful when she works her energy at a slow and consistent pace. When she gets flustered and begins to flow with an uneven rhythm, she makes impulsive decisions and scolds herself for it all day and night.

Because she has low self-worth she tends to be walked all over by herself and others. When she is in a state of low self-worth she will do anything to please others, and she will do anything to be accepted. When she finally decides to love herself she will no longer be walked on by others and her creative side will come flooding out of her.

Her creative side is an absolute delight, and when she is confident and comfortable with herself it will be released. The confidence that it takes for her creativity to show is the same quality that will allow her to productively navigate love. When she is confident and she realizes how beautiful she really is, she is able to pick the right match for her energy.

When she finds that perfect match she will not feel the need to rush the relationship, as she will be comfortable in allowing the love to take its course. When that occurs the opportunity for long-lasting love flourishes.

Finding the confidence to move at her own pace will allow the Virgo woman to navigate her emotions and her life. This power is the key to her success throughout her life. As an earth sign, the Virgo woman carries the weight of the world with her. Because of this, when she can exert that immense energetic weight with purpose she will create peace and harmony for herself.

Libra Man

The Libra man is one of the most unique guys within the Zodiac. Because is an air sign, his thoughts are constantly flying around his head, ever-changing.

The Libra sign is represented by a scale, while all the other Zodiacs are either an animal or a human being. Right away you can see how the energy of a Libra is very unique, as it is an object that can go up or down in either direction, and mostly every other Zodiac finds the Libra rather amusing.

All of the other Zodiacs are most familiar with signs that resonate with animals and human beings, and as a result, and a sign that resembles something other than that draws a great deal of attention.

It is important for the Libra man to recognize that he is always being observed by others, so he must be sure to always have high integrity. He must also remember not to judge himself, as many times Libra is extremely goofy and can come off as foolish or aloof.

The Libra man is easy to spot. Whether he is big and burly or small and skinny, he usually wears a childlike, chubby-cheeked smile. Libras are also very funny and knowledgeable, always spitting out fun facts or other types of jokes that will make people laugh. Similarly to how a scale operates, they can swing from happy to sad within one instant. This sway is more often than not caused by their own highly critical thought process.

As an air sign, his energy field is constantly fluttering like the wings of a hummingbird. In addition, he is also very in tune with and aware of his surroundings. This awareness causes him to judge himself in relation to how he acts in all situations. The key remedy for this is acceptance, because when he decides to accept and love himself and his life he is able to create with unlimited potential.

The creativity that lies inherently within every Libra will inevitably free him from his own mental prison. When the Libra stops trying to force his life into a certain trajectory that he sees as perfect, his life will develop organically and beautifully.

It is also important for him to take some of the weight off of the right side of the scale, because when he distributes energy to the left side he will be harmoniously in balance.

Creativity brings Libra men an abundance of joy. When they are truly happy and carefree everybody that they come into contact with enjoys them and even craves them. The Libra man will find that his positive energy is infectious and that others will be very grateful to receive his attention.

This acknowledgement of the power of his positive energy is important to remember when he goes into a relationship. Many times Libra men will be lured into a relationship because the other person craves a piece of the Libra's creative confidence. This can become very draining for the Libra and could even lead him into depression or spells of negativity.

It is important for him to identify and understand what exactly it is that he wants, what type of energy he enjoys. Once he has this information he can properly seek out the right match. As an air sign, he moves very quickly and swiftly and, because of this, his match will have to be on the same page. If this is not the case the relationship is not likely to flourish.

The Libra man is capable of great things, and when he is truly confident in allowing his fun and creative side to show, he will be most successful. Until this occurs, he will perpetuate low self-worth with over-critical thoughts that will many times drive him crazy. He must begin by not judging himself, and from there he will be able to also refrain from judging other people and his surroundings. Once he finally lives without judgment he will find true harmony, and a harmonious match will find him.

Libra Woman

The Libra woman is one of the strongest and most intelligent women of the Zodiac. With that being said, it is important that these women remain humble. Whether her elegant beauty catches people's eyes, or her competitive leadership skills draw attention, the Libra lady is very powerful.

In her youth, however, she is many times over-looked, and this leads her to feel as if she needs to get her point across aggressively. She carries a strong and intelligent energy and, because of this, she can come off as intimidating or judgmental. This can lead her to become apathetic about life because she wants to prove that she can be relaxed. This can lead her into some serious trouble. It is imperative for the Libra lady to find balance with her emotions.

Libra women aren't hard to spot, as they have beautiful eyes with eyelashes that grab your attention immediately. Once she has your attention it's almost as if you're at her mercy, as she is very in tune with others and she may seem like a mind reader.

Her hyper-awareness picks up your every thought through body language and energy. Her natural intuition makes her very smart and confident in herself.

This confidence is very powerful once she is able to sustain it. Her sign is represented by a scale and, because of this, if she is unable to sustain her confidence, she is likely to swing up and down upon her scale, displaying a tidal wave of emotions.

Understanding that she is very smart and that she has a dominant energy will allow her to feel confident unconditionally. She will begin to believe in herself, and with that belief she will feel much more comfortable accepting life for what it is. When she accepts herself and her surroundings, she will no longer feel the need to judge and attempt to change herself.

When she can learn to accept things as perfectly imperfect she will be able to see the beauty in life, thus leading her to a more blissful daily approach. When she carries that blissful approach she is much easier to be around and people are more likely to want to work with her, which is something that she values greatly.

She very much wants a team-oriented lifestyle from work to family. In essence, she wants everybody to get along, and she wants the ship to move quickly. This can only happen, however, when she, the captain, is not a slave driver and is more of an informative tour guide.

This same concept applies when it comes to her love life, as she must accept herself first before she can accept any partner. If she does not accept herself, she will be highly judgmental of anything her partner does, and she will eventually drive them away. Many times her insecurities or lack of confidence can cause emotional swings.

It is important for her to be confident in who she is and embrace all sides of herself, including the fun side and the work side. When she begins to feel confident in a balanced emotional state of mind she is usually is able to attract a partner with ease. If she continues within an off-balanced state she will continue to attract unproductive relationships.

She must trust and believe in herself, and this will allow the Libra lady to find great peace in her life. Her desire to be accepted will be met when she accepts her life for what it is. When she is able to navigate her emotions in a positive way and she is able to find balance between work and play, she will cultivate stability in her life.

When she finds this stability she will be able to choose which energy she wishes to engage with quite easily. When she engages with the appropriate energy she will cultivate a fun, long-lasting relationship.

Scorpio Man

The Scorpio man is one of the more mysterious men in the Zodiac. He is tough to get through to, and if you do succeed in getting through to him, you may not be receiving the truth, as Scorpios can be great liars. Life is truly a mystery for them, and they are always seeking a great epiphany. This is where their mysterious quality comes from.

Because they are constantly searching for a higher purpose, they will many times heavily indulge in any aspect of life that they perceive as fitting in any particular moment. This overindulgence may cause them to seek validation externally, relying on others to provide them with a sense of value rather than cultivating self-worth. When they realize that their self-worth comes from inside of themselves, they will no longer feel the need to jump from external source to external source. When this occurs the right partner will also come into their lives.

On the outside they are usually tall, dark and handsome, but beneath the surface lies a nervous boy, lost in his own self-doubt. The Scorpio man can spend too much of his time and energy attempting to be cool while keeping himself unknown to the outside world. This prevents him from discovering what he is truly passionate about.

As a result, when the Scorpio man finally summons up the courage to show the world who he truly is, he is not sure what to tell the world because he hasn't really gotten to know himself yet. Because of this, he will latch onto an image of what others think he should be, and he placates to this.

The key for this guy is to go with the flow. Scorpios are water signs, and it is imperative that they keep this in mind. Water can flow at any pace, fast or slow, and it is important for the Scorpio man to discover the pace at which he enjoys flowing. By discovering this he will also be able to understand what truly stimulates him. Many times he will start an endeavor because he is seeking validation from others and he wants to fit in. The fear of the unknown is huge for this guy, and this fear can leave him stagnant.

When he has cultivated the ability to let go of negative energies while staying confident that he can create his own more positive energies at his own will, he will find peace and harmony in his life. With this newfound peace and harmony he will attract a partner who flows similarly to him.

When he is channeling positive energy he will create a newfound sense of self-worth, as self-worth can only be created from the inside. With this self-worth will come a great deal of confidence that will attract the perfect match for him.

Rest assured that you are as great as you strive to be, Scorpio man. When this confidence settles in, make sure that you take the time to appreciate the world around you. Immerse yourself in many different arenas, as you have unlimited potential to excel. While engaging in one of those arenas you will find your perfect partner. This partner will only come into your life after you have first and foremost cultivated your own self-value.

Scorpio Woman

The Scorpio woman, a water sign, is a very powerful and smart woman. What makes her so powerful is her ability to manipulate anyone with just a passing glance. This power can be a gift and a curse for her.

Many times she can get caught up in using others for her own benefit while creating negative energy for herself. Other times she can be very bossy and have a difficult time connecting to others when she is trying to help them. It is important for her to use her intuition and intelligence with grace. When she is graceful and kind she is able to channel very positive energy.

Insecurities such as jealousy can influence her to be very manipulative. Once she has found confidence in herself, the strong, powerful match that she longs for will come her way.

The Scorpio woman usually has a very seductive energy. It is this seductive quality that is her gift and also her curse in life. She is usually able to get what she wants by using her words and body language to convey a clear message. This power that she has to manipulate can sometimes be difficult for her to handle and, because of this, she may use this power in negative ways.

When she is young she many times feels insecure about herself, and she worries about her popularity. In response to this, she can many times create gossip amongst her friends. She is very doubtful of herself, and this can lead her to jump from relationship to relationship in search for a cure for her self-doubt.

Finding her true self-worth will come from immersing herself into something that fully engages all of her strength and intuition. When she comes to this understanding she will no longer feel the need for outside approval.

Once the Scorpio lady has a good sense of confidence and self-worth, she is unstoppable. When she really comes into her power she often comes off as intimidating to her peers. With all of this power she can become overbearing and bossy and, because of this, it is important for her to take control with grace and confidence.

When she really sits back and observes the situation from a calmer perspective, she will gain greater control of the direction she is headed.

As a water sign, it is important for her to be able have intentional direction over her life. When this comes into fruition every component of her life will fall into place.

The partner of her dreams will most certainly be on the same wavelength as her. Because she is so strong and smart, whoever will walk by her side must be in good shape. She is strong in her desires, and most of the time it's her way or the highway.

She wants power to be generated from her relationships. If there is no power generated she feels that she's just better off creating power by herself.

In order for her to find the perfect partner she must gain immaculate control of her energy and how it flows. When she cultivates this control, somebody that is on the same wavelength will cross her path, and she will know without a doubt that she has found that person.

There is nothing that a Scorpio woman cannot do when she has settled into herself. She must trust herself, and by doing this she will bring about great confidence. When she is careful not to lead with an iron fist, she is able to move on with ease and grace.

Sagittarius Man

The Sagittarius man is one of the more macho men in the Zodiac. As a fire sign, he is passionate and powerful and enjoys being in control of whatever he chooses to do.

His sign is represented by a centaur, which is half-man, half-horse. This is the only Zodiac that is half human and half animal. This uniqueness translates into a uniqueness in the energy that they exude in their everyday lives. Because of this, they interact with the world differently, and this helps them in accomplishing their dreams.

The Sagittarius man truly stands out, and frequently translates into over-confidence. They are often perceived as rude and are disconnected from their feelings. They won't truly experience love until they can comfortably tap into their sensitive sides.

To spot a Sagittarius man just look for the guy who looks like he's on the football team. Most Sagittarius men have strong, manly builds, and this is usually where their confidence derives from.

This confidence from a young age can lead others to find them arrogant or rude, but it is just in their nature to believe in themselves. Because they are naturally confident, it is important for them to learn how to lead by setting an example with their actions, by not bragging or believing that they are better than anybody else.

As a fire sign, he knows how to spark interest in others and, because of this, he is loved by his community. Because he is over-confident, however, he can lose people in his life very quickly.

Finding a humble approach to life is key for Sagittarius men. When they have found success in their fields of choice, they are known to truly dominate. Many times they tend to be bullies, and because they are successful, they don't realize how detrimental it can be to those around them.

The Sagittarius man has no problem approaching his life with this mindset of domination no matter who is in his way. True joy, however, lies within his creative and sensitive side. Because he is so strong and dominant, once he taps into his sensitive side his potential increases exponentially. In essence, he becomes whole, and he uncovers his true power that he may have never imagined before.

This power that comes from combining his strength with his sensitivity is what will eventually attract his perfect match. When the Sagittarius man has not tapped into his sensitive side, he gives away his energy to a slew of relationships that only exist because they validate his ego. Rarely does he ever experience true and pure love, but when he opens up into sensitivity, the ability to love is revealed. Because he naturally attracts partners so easily, he certainly won't have any trouble finding the right one.

Life truly is in your control, Sagittarius man, but you must avoid being too confident and too powerful for your own good. You will find a feeling of power you have never imagined once you allow yourself to feel openly. Embrace the sensations of the softer side of life and allow the positive energy to come rushing inside of you. Use your fire to illuminate others, not burn to them.

Sagittarius Woman

The Sagittarius woman is one of the most exciting and energetic women in the Zodiac. She is extremely intelligent and very aware of her abilities. As a fire sign, she is always full of energy and passion and is always ready to attack whatever task is in front of her.

All of this energy can backfire for the Sagittarius lady, as she can be prone to getting overwhelmed, which many times leads her to having low self-esteem and doubt.

Growing up in a household with parents who compete with one another can leave this young lady to fend for herself in her early years. This allows the Sagittarius woman to traverse life on her own. A string of mistakes may come her way, but after she learns how to properly assert herself she is bound for success.

In the arena of love she is sure to find a match that stirs up her fire in a powerful way, but only when she knows the intensity of her own fire. She must learn to master her own powerful energy before she can have any success letting anybody close to it.

From the time she develops a sense of the world, the Sagittarius woman is capable of amazing things. She has beauty, intelligence, creativity, and strength from a very young age. Many Sagittarius women are even known to become professionals at a young age. This is because they have harnessed self-confidence in their fields of choice. Sagittarius women that are unable to cultivate self-confidence commonly develop hyperanxieties and tend to display low self-esteem.

It is important for Sagittarius women to remember that their sign is represented by a centaur, a half-human half-horse being that rides around with a bow and arrow on its back. The centaur is very powerful and skilled.

Sagittarius women have the ability to hit any target they choose, but they must understand that they can only hit one target at a time.

Frequently they overwhelm themselves by attempting to do too many things at once.

The key for these women is to take life one step at a time. Since they are so skilled they are capable of achieving success with every step. Because of this, the ability to attack life in this fashion will provide them with success at all times.

When she has harnessed the fire inside of her and has learned how to properly attack each situation, she will feel extremely self-assured and self-confident.

Once she begins to carry herself with high self-worth, the sky's the limit for the Sagittarius lady. She is known to attract a great deal of attention and wealth, so they will both come pouring into her reality once she believes in who she is.

As this confidence allows abundance into her life, the ability to find the right match will also present itself. When this fire sign is off-balance and over-aggressive, her fire can be too hot for whomever she shares it with. She commonly engages in highly dramatic relationships that tend to go down in flames, and this is because she is not in control of her power, her fire.

Because she is so beautiful, charming and smart, anyone she chooses will gladly enter her life. If they are not ready to handle her fire, however, she is quick to call them out for it. This leads both parties to feel upset, which creates arguments and eventually causes the two to separate. Because of this, when she gains control of her fire, she is able to attract another individual who is also in control of their power. When she meets somebody that has the same level of self-control that she has, the two of them will create amazing things together.

The sky is limit for the Sagittarius woman, but only when she relaxes, takes a moment to gather herself and then delivers her amazing energy to the world. Attempting to do too many things at once will slow her process down and cause her to feel frustrated and hopeless.

Enjoying each moment one at a time will bring her great clarity and self-confidence. With this self-confidence she is able to properly work her energy which will effortlessly draw success, love, and abundance to her.

Capricorn Man

The Capricorn man is one of the most calm and collected men within the Zodiac. He is more often than not very reserved, and he keeps to himself. They are natural homebodies, and are also very family-oriented.

As an earth sign, they like to move at their own pace, which can sometimes lead them into lazy habits. The Capricorn man can get too comfortable with his life, which can sometimes lead him to not live up to his full potential. It is important for the Capricorn man to realize how amazing his energy truly is and where it can take him. Many Capricorn men are so fearful of change and new horizons that they spend their whole lives in one comfortable place.

From a young age the Capricorn man wants to be accepted and feel a family-like connection to his group of friends. His laid back and go-with-the-flow personality is loved by those around him, so it is easy for him to become very popular.

Usually built with strength, these men are notorious for being talented in sports, and if it is not sports that calls to them, another form of creativity will come to them.

They love to tinker with things, often becoming mechanics or builders. With that being said, they usually find their niche and set up shop. It takes a lot of push to get the Capricorn man to leave his hometown nest. This is because in his mind, he has already put in the time and effort to grow in the space that he is already in, and he doesn't want to have to start from scratch.

This desire to stay within his comfort zone is what can prevent the Capricorn man from reaching his full potential. Although staying at home isn't necessarily negative, it many times leads the Capricorn man to develop a lazy and lethargic habitual pattern.

In truth, he is very talented and is capable of many things. He will be much more successful if he leaves the nest and takes on the world anew.

Many times he will get used to this routine of simply doing just enough to get by, while finishing his day at the local pub with his friends.

It is important for the Capricorn man to remember that we only live this life once and, because of this, it is important for us to have the strength inside of ourselves to take on change and new challenges. He must remember that he can always return to his hometown and that his family and friends will still be there waiting for him. It is so important for him to find the courage inside of himself to take risks and open himself to new opportunities.

This same concept applies for him when it comes to love as well. He is very strong, cool and fun to be around, but because he has a lack of drive, and because he easily falls back into what is comfortable for him, disharmony in his relationships may arise. It is important for him to find spontaneity and for him to keep things fresh in his love life.

The Capricorn man must not allow his personal routine to integrate its way into his romantic life. His tendency to stay cool and calm is great, but when he is also fresh and exciting he can be even more appealing. When he is able to integrate all of these qualities and he is able to stay true to himself, the perfect match will cross his path.

The Capricorn man is a great and powerful earth sign, but like the earth, he must let his rivers run out of the country woods and into the great oceans. When this occurs he will be able to find a balance of strength that will aid him in developing his abilities and courage. This will allow them to flourish outside of his home roots. When he finds this balance his perfect match will flow directly to him with ease and grace, and he will also find the family he has longed for since his youth.

Capricorn Woman

The Capricorn woman is strong, beautiful and very fun to be around. Throughout her life and especially as a child she is very focused on her own agenda, how to properly accomplish the goals on her mental list.

As an earth sign, her family and friends are very important to her, and many times she is caught between her needs and the needs of her friends and family.

With the desire to be accepted she becomes very easy-going in order to get along with everyone. Unfortunately, this can backfire on the smart Capricorn woman because she will be quick to realize when she is getting the short end of the stick. When that light bulb goes off in her head she becomes fierce and focused on herself, leaving some friends and family wondering where this suddenly bold women came from. Ironically, she has been there the entire time, the Capricorn is now just allowing this to shine.

In her youth the Capricorn woman is an intelligent ball of energy, filled with curiosity and excitement that makes her a joy to be around. She is eager to make connections and have a group of friends that are very much like a family, and as a result, when she first becomes social, she is very easy going.

As she grows older and begins to develop who she is and what she wants, she becomes much more goal-oriented. This is because she realizes what she needs to do in order to create success in her life. The challenge begins when her close friends and family don't share the same passion for their own lives. The Capricorn woman has so much drive and, because of this, she has the courage to leave her old ways. It is important for her to do this with grace and with a smile on her face.

Many times the Capricorn woman is involved in some sort of office relationship that tends to create drama in her life. This can be because the people around her are jealous of her highly driven and passionate energy. The drama can also arise because she hasn't fully expressed her wants and needs consistently throughout her life and is now attempting to do that all at once. This volcanic explosion of wants and needs is not healthy for her, as her energy is too strong to unload so much at one time.

It is important for her to communicate with the people in her life once she sees the path to reaching her goal. This will prevent resentment when she swiftly makes her move to the next challenge on her road to success.

On the other hand, she can also find herself engaging with drama because of a lack of drive and passion. Due to insecurities and self-doubt she can also be very laid-back and unfocused. Because of this, she commonly parties her way into unsuccessful experiences. It is very important for her to have a balance of work and play, as too much of one can lead to poor energetic flow for the Capricorn lady.

In the arena of love she must watch out for the same problem. She must allow her strong business mind to handle the business side of love, not the romantic side. Having the confidence and courage to show her emotions instead of trying to plan out the relationship will allow her and her partner to really enjoy each other in an organic way.

Trouble only finds her when she is trying to force the relationship in a certain direction. Doing this can lead the Capricorn woman to resent her partner for not putting in as much effort as she is. This can also lead her partner to resent her for being over-aggressive and pushy.

Balance is key for the Capricorn woman. When she is able to use her strong business mind for good and use her fun and playful side for love and adventure, she will attract great positive energy. With that positive energy she is capable of achieving anything that she sets her mind to.

This positive state comes from balancing herself. With a balanced self she will be able to attract the perfect match and when that happens, a balanced self is what will keep the relationship thriving.

Part III:
The Code to Your Soul for The Mind

The mind is the most unique and powerful gift that our physical body is given. It is able to create, organize, and manipulate our perspectives on what we experience in each and every moment. Learning about the energy in numbers will result in a better understanding of yourself and your relationships with others.

The reason that each of us has particular thought processes and habitual patterns of thinking largely has to do with our date of birth. When the numbers in our dates of birth are added together and are inserted into different formulas, we can gather a huge amount of information about why we are the way that we are and how the energy that we were given at birth contributes to that. Our date of birth creates a unique framework of thought that is specific for every single person. Each number represents certain characteristics that create and affect the way that we experience everyday life.

You'll soon discover that as awareness expands, your understanding of each and every relationship you share with others will become more clear. The key to achieving a heightened sense of clarity is to remain aware of the fact that no two individuals will be the same, even if they are born on the same day.

Ultimately, each and every one of us will be products of our respective environments. Although you may share the same numbers and certain similarities with others, there will still be tendencies from each number that are more prevalent inside of you that are the exact opposite for others. As your understanding grows, you'll be able to trace where your emotions stem from and use this knowledge to eliminate negative thought patterns.

An important law to be aware of is "*whatever energy you put out with your thoughts and actions will inevitably come back to you.*"

With this in mind, the more you create positive outcomes on a daily basis, the better you and those around you will feel. As creatures of habit, this process helps us break old, unhealthy, confrontational and negative tendencies. These are then replaced with positive, productive, and open-minded perspectives. As more people expand their awareness, misunderstandings will inevitably fade and a more harmonious and peaceful reality will be available for all to enjoy together.

The Code to Your Soul Explained

The Code to Your Soul is a revolutionary system and understanding of the energy that all human beings were given at birth, specific to the date on which they were born.

There are three different applications for CTYS and, when fully comprehended and applied, they will bring clarity to your everyday awareness.

The first application is to acknowledge the characteristics of each number. The second application is to learn the structure of the system of energy that the numbers relate to. The final application is to understand the four components of the energy system.

The characteristics of each number are distinctive to the title of each specific field of energy.

Numbers 1, 3, 5, and 7 all consist of a heightened awareness to energy and an extensive ability to feel and think deeply about life.

Numbers 2, 4, 6, and 8 are fundamental structural base energies that build our core value systems and our habitual patterns of behavior.

Number 9 is unique because it holds aspects of both structure and feeling, which amplifies everything around it.

Lastly, 0 represents a possession of an inner gift, and it brings a unique quality to any arena in which it exists.

The structure of energy exists on three levels, all of which work in conjunction with one another.

The first and most prominent level is the **Emotional Core.** This component is what our bodies and minds feel as our lives takes their courses from moment to moment.

The second component is the **Ruling Energy**, which consists of what we're looking for in life and what governs our minds' perception of what it is experiencing. This component changes halfway through our lives at a specific age tailored to the emotional energy that you inhabited at birth.

The third component is created out of both the Emotional Core and the Ruling Energy and is known as the **Point of Creation.** This energy field consists of the connection of the Ruling Energy and Emotional Core energies creating an avenue to how we create our reality. As the human mind begins to expands its awareness of how these three fields work in unison, a greater clarity is present for them to thrive and grow.

The final application is the ability to apply all of this knowledge to the four specific arenas of our lives that these number characteristics and energy structures affect every single day.

The first arena is **inside of yourself**, where you possess energies at each of the three energetic levels. This helps individuals recognize their inherited strengths while also becoming aware of their weaknesses and which aspects of themselves may need to be corrected for a healthier state of mind.

The second arena consists of **cycles of growth**, which happen emotionally through our experiences, creating processes for us to grow individually. This helps each person have a higher understanding of where he or she stands in life and how to attack the moment to its fullest potential.

The third arena consists of **our relationships and connections** with each other within our emotions, experiences, and collective creations. This arena is our greatest tool for understanding the frequencies between each and every person which helps us create less confrontation because we're aware of why people react a certain way toward particular individuals.

The final arena encompasses an energy that is consistent with **the specific day** that we are experiencing together as a collective. It is a universally represented energy that is affected at each level, which is consistent with the specific day that we are all collectively experiencing. This helps us recognize why certain energies are more prevalent on specific days, allowing each of us to attack that particular day to our fullest potential no matter what the energy is and how it might be affecting us.

What follows next is a breakdown of how each field of energy is calculated along with the characteristics of each number and the arenas in which they're presented.

We would also like to add that every part of this system is consistent mathematically in a number of different ways, proving that this is a very real concept.

Identifying the Energies within Numbers

0 – Inner Gifts

In our universe we have curved lines and straight lines. A curved line is represented as feminine, and a straight line is represented as masculine.

On top of all the information that we have uncovered about the numbers we have also taken notice of the energy of their physical appearances. The number 0 is our first feminine number, as it is composed of one big curved line.

Another way to distinguish which numbers are masculine and which numbers are feminine is by identifying what is particle (what you can see) and what is matrix, (what you cannot see). The particle is masculine and the matrix is feminine.

Therefore, if you look at 0, you can see that it consists of a single curved line that is holding a ball of energy inside of it that we cannot see. The number 0 literally holds an inner gift inside of it.

0 is an enhancer, as it holds the unseen power of life inside of it. When a 0 is next to any other number it greatly enhances the traits of that number.

1 – Creativity and Confidence

The number 1 is simply a straight line and, because of this, it carries a masculine energy.

Since 0 is feminine and 1 is masculine, together they are our creator numbers. This gives us insight into why binary code, the coding that makes up our computers consists of 1s and 0s.

The number 1 is all about pure creation in the masculine form. On the other hand, 0 is working with the energy that is unseen, that must be believed in.

The number 1 creates the entire physical world that surrounds you. Because of this, those who carry a 1 with them have an enormous ability to create. Good creation, however, evolves when people have great confidence in themselves.

Those who carry a 1 with them must be mindful of staying confident at all times, as they can be prone to swinging in and out of confidence. When they have low confidence, their insecurities are loud.

Since the number 1 is a masculine energy and is the most raw form that a number can be in, those that carry this number with them can be highly competitive, always attempting to beat their opponents and present their immense abilities to create.

This highly competitive nature can be helpful in some circumstances, but when it is out of their control, their strong energies can be difficult for some to interact with. It is important for those working with the number 1 to understand that 1 acts as an energy channel, so for these individuals, energy moves through them like water through a fishnet.

Whatever they choose to indulge themselves in will affect them greatly because they have very vibrant energy fields. It is important for individuals carrying this number to keep their bodies loose and in shape. Our energy usually travels through our spines and, because of this, if these individuals do not allow their energy to flow without blockages they can have serious back problems.

Since 1 is an energy channel, it is able to pick up on all aspects of life and, because of this, it is important for those working with the number

1 to stay active and engage with many different things, as becoming stagnant can destroy their creative flows and can also lead them into spells of low confidence.

2 – Cooperation and Balance

The number 2 is our first bisexual number. When we talk about sexuality we are discussing the energy of the number, not sexual orientation.

If you look at the number 2, it has both curved lines and straight lines. Because the 2 has both feminine and masculine qualities, we can understand that it has a bisexual energy.

In addition, the two numbers before 2 alternate in a pattern of first feminine and then masculine. After the number 2, this pattern continues up until number 5. The feminine and masculine energies that make up the number 2 are actually aligned with the traits that number 2 has.

It is important for those who are working with the number 2 to stay balanced within their energy, since the number holds feminine and masculine energies. Staying too much in one energy will leave whomever works with the number 2 very stressed.

Because the balance is off, this can draw resentment toward yourself from those around you because they feel that you are not willing to meet them halfway. This resentment that you receive from others is just a reflection of the subconscious resentment that you have toward yourself because you are continuously living off-balanced. Balance yourself, and your world will balance with you.

3 – Expression and Sensitivity

As we discussed earlier, the number 3 is a feminine number because it has curved lines. It is not surprising that expression and sensitivity is a feminine energy, as those qualities are usually associated with femininity.

For those that have the number 3 in their codes, it is very important that they express themselves. The way in which that expression is channeled is up to the individual, but expression is key.

If these individuals block their expression, they have the potential to become over-sensitive to others. Many 3s will cease to express all together and, because of this, it can be very difficult to communicate with them.

On the other hand, 3s can be over-expressive because they are looking for attention. When this powerful number realizes that the attention that they seek will come from having faith in their own self-expression, this will greatly clarify and harmonize their realities.

When they are in balance they have the ability to be very receptive to others' emotions. They tend to become hyper-sensitive to body language, tone and touch.

When working with this number in a productive way, these individuals have the ability to help others control their emotions.

4 – Stability and Process

By observing the straight lines that the number 4 possesses we can see that this is our second masculine number. In addition, you can also see that the number looks very stabilized, as if it were the foundation for another number to build upon.

While working with the number 4, this quality is key. It is imperative for 4s to build a strong foundation and go from there.

The masculine energy that the number possesses aligns with its natural characteristics. Masculine energies have the ability to figure out how to dominate and be successful in this reality. Because of this, those working with 4 have a wonderful ability to see the road to success.

If they skip steps and do not stay on course while following their process, they will hit roadblocks and potholes that will inevitably send them back to square one.

For those that carry a 4, it is important for them to understand that their energy is capable of being an extremely strong foundation for themselves and those around them.

If they do not take the time to build that foundation, a collapse is bound to occur. A collapse of a tall building can be a very dramatic event and, because of this, people have the potential to have a lot of drama in their lives if they are unstable.

Creating a strong and stable foundation will give them the confidence to build their dreams high into the sky without having to worry that it will come crashing down.

5 – Freedom and Discipline

By observing the curved and straight lines we can see that the number 5 is our second bisexual number. The number 5 is also representative of the human connection.

Five is all about freedom and discipline, and those that work with the number 5 must balance these two qualities. Because 5 is representative of the human being, everybody is able to relate to these individuals. As a result of this, everybody always wants to surround themselves with anybody who carries a 5, as they enjoy the social interaction.

Although this human connection is beautiful, many times individuals working with the number 5 spend too much of their time interacting with other people while neglecting to be disciplined with themselves, taking care of their own lives.

When those working with the number 5 cultivate discipline they will find success. Through this success they will find freedom.

The number 5 also represents speed and change, and as a result they tend to move quickly from project to project, as they don't want to be "bored." It is essential for them to find direction where they can incorporate their human connection.

Many 5s are great at working with their hands, as they release a lot of energy that way. These individuals also really enjoy engaging in projects that are hands-on.

Once this group of people find activities that they enjoy they must be careful not to over-indulge in these activities, as they always need to focus on having a balance within their lives. The bisexual numbers always need to focus on creating balance.

6 – Vision and Acceptance

The numbers 6 and 9 are very unique in nature. Our first six numbers (0, 1, 2, 3, 4, and 5) carried a pattern; feminine, masculine, bi, feminine, masculine, bi. Now, we only have four numbers left (6, 7, 8, and 9).

You may notice that 6 and 9 are the same figure just flipped upside down. These numbers are the bookends for the numbers 7 and 8, the biggest energetic masculine and feminine numbers there are.

6 and 9 are both bisexual, but these four numbers are unique and different from the previous six numbers in terms of their energy.

Sixes are very intelligent and are very good at analyzing the world around them. However, because they are very hyper-aware, they can also be very judgmental of themselves and others.

For them to be successful, it is important for them to accept themselves and other people.

Those working with the number 6 are going to be different. They are many times perceived as "weird" or "freaky," and because of this, they might attract attention and criticism.

For them to find happiness they must allow life to flow naturally. The more they attempt to critique and fix the world around them, the more they spin their wheels.

When they are able to accept everything as being perfectly imperfect, they are able to visualize and create amazing things. Through these visions, they are able to create success with a smile on their faces without any judgment.

7 – Trust and Openness

The number 7 is the last masculine number, as you can see by observing its straight lines.

The number 7 is a perfect example of a masculine energy. It is extremely wise and full of knowledge, but if uninterested, it will shut off completely and become very difficult for anybody to connect with.

Although they have vast amounts of knowledge and information, 7s are not confident in their knowledge bases. Because they are not confident with their own knowledge and intelligence, they want to share their information with everybody in an attempt to prove their intellects.

These are some of the aspects of the number 7 that have the potential to come off as very clingy, as 7s often need a lot of reassurance. What is important for this number is to trust themselves and know that they are very wise.

Sevens are deeply connected to the heavens. Because of this, there is a great amount of information that these individuals have to share with the world. It is important for them to be open, while remembering not to shut themselves off from the world because they believe that they are better than anybody else.

Sevens very much enjoy having a meaningful purpose in their lives and, because of this, it is important for them to use their great knowledge for good, by helping and teaching others, and also by trusting and believing that the universe is working in their favor. Essentially, it's important for a 7 to remember that if a door closes that they particularly wanted to explore, there is a great chance that the next door to open will be better than the one that they had previously desired.

8 – Abundance and Recognition

The number 8 is our last feminine number built from two circles sitting on top of one another. This feminine energy is perfect for understanding how to work with the number 8. Since feminine energy is focused on the energy we cannot see, we must believe that it is there.

Eights are going to be recognized, and they will draw attention to them wherever they go. Because of this, the key for them is to not to grab this attention. When 8s push at people and try to snatch their attention, they can come off as overwhelming to others.

Practicing humbleness will help 8s immensely. An aggressive feminine energy is tough for others to handle and, because of this, engaging in a delightful, humble approach is key.

They must learn to walk with quiet confidence and trust that an abundance of recognition is coming their way. The less they push their massive energy outwardly, the more the outside energies are drawn to them.

9 – Wisdom and Integrity

The number 9 is our last bisexual number. As we have stated before, 6 and 9 are the same number flipped upside down. They are also bookends for our last two numbers, 7 and 8.

Nine, like 6, needs to understand that its energy is unique and is most certainly on a different wavelength than other numbers.

Nines act as mirrors to any number with which they come into contact. For example, if someone is a 4 and has a relationship with a 9, the number makes 13. 1 + 3 is 4, so the result would be a 13/4. This is why 9 is a mirror. It does this for every number.

With 9 being a bisexual number, it has a great responsibility to maintain balance. It is important to understand that, yes, 9s are filled with great wisdom and are on a different page than many others, but they are also mirrors for everyone. Because of this, everyone feels a familiarity with a 9.

This means that 9s must harbor great integrity when working with others. It is important not to kick others to the curb because they are a few pages behind you.

Nines can be amazing leaders, but they have to take the time to lead. Some 9s get frustrated trying to lead with their words. Teaching does not come naturally to some 9s, so for them the key is learning to lead through example. When 9s can peacefully lead by example, there is nothing that can stop them from being successful.

Calculating Your Numbers

Emotional Core

Emotional Core (EC) consists of 1, 3, or 5 digits that influence the emotions that you feel and exude in your energy field. These numbers directly affect your daily thoughts and feelings that you project outwardly.

Becoming aware of these energies gives the individual the opportunity to create a better understanding of who he is and what his personal strengths are, as well as where his weaknesses lie.

It also presents individuals with the ability to understand how others think and feel, giving them a better understanding of those around them, and how to communicate with them most effectively.

How to Calculate:

1. Add up all the individual digits associated with your complete date of birth. When you receive an outcome that is more than one digit, this represents the first number that makes up your emotional core.

> ***Example:*** *Birthday – 3/15/1954*
>
> 3 + 1 + 5 + 1 + 9 + 5 + 4 = **28**
>
> This is the first number in your emotional core.

2. When you add these digits together, you receive the second number that makes up your emotional core. The second

number is most significant in that it represents your emotional core overall.

> ***Example continued:***
>
> `2 + 8 = 10`
>
> This is the second number in your emotional core.

3. If the second number is not a single digit number, we add them together again to get the third number in your emotional core. (In our example, we'll have a 5-digit EC when we're done. Depending on the numbers being added for your birth date, you may only have a 1 or 3-digit EC.)

> ***Example continued:***
>
> `1 + 0 = 1`
>
> This is the third number in your emotional core.

Based on our example, you can see that the birth date 3/15/1954 has a 5-digit EC that is written as 28/10/1.

The first two numbers that are added up to create the second number (in our example, 2 and 8) are also important because they impact the dynamic of the second number. For example, 31 and 22 both equal 4 as an emotional core, but the ingredients that create the 4 are different and, therefore, the 4s that are created by the 31 and the 22 are not the same.

Ruling Energy

Ruling Energy (RE) consists of 1, 3 or 5 digits and describes the energy that the individual is experiencing within her reality. Essentially, the Ruling Energy encompasses how the world perceives you and explains why you are perceived this way.

It also has to do with how the energy within your environment affects you. This number changes halfway through your life, which is determined based on the emotional energy that you were born into.

Breaking through to understanding this field of energy gives the individual the ability to recognize his actions and why he may always find himself in similar predicaments. Gaining awareness of this will help the individual in his efforts to create a more positive life for himself.

How to Calculate:

1. Add up all of the individual digits of your month and day of birth for the first half of your life.

> *Example: Birthday – 3/15/1954*
>
> **3 + 1 + 5 = 9**
>
> This number represents the ruling energy for the first half of your life.

2. Add each digit of the year for the second half of your life, and continue adding the new numbers until you get to a single digit.

> ***Example continued:***
>
> **1 + 9 + 5 + 4 = 19**
> **1 + 9 = 10**
> **1 + 0 = 1**
>
> This number combination (19/10/1) represents the ruling energy for second half of your life.

Point of Creation

Point of Creation (PoC) consists of 1 or 3 digits and is found when your Emotional Core intersects with your Ruling Energy. When these two energies connect, the Point of Creation is how you channel these energies to affect your reality.

This component allows each individual to understand how she can utilize her birth-given energies, Emotional Core and Ruling Energy, optimally to create the reality that she envisions for herself. This concept draws parallels to the Law of Attraction, so it is more specific to each individual.

When the Point of Creation is focused on and manifested on pure intentions, it is the most powerful strength in our consciousness. The Point of Creation cannot be engaged with in a way that is optimal to each human being unless that individual fully comprehends his Ruling Energy and Point of Creation and has honed his interaction with each of these energies.

How to Calculate:

1. Add the last number of your Ruling Energy to the last number of your Emotional Core. Because your Ruling Energy shifts halfway through your life, so does your Point of Creation. Therefore, to get the Point of Creation for the first half of your life, add your Ruling Energy for the first half of your life to your Emotional Core.

***Example:** Birthday – 3/15/1954*

For the first half of life, the RE was 9. So we'll take that and add it to the last number of the EC, which was 28/10/1, and continue to solve until we get a single digit.

9 + 1 = 10

1 + 0 = 1

So, the PoC for the first half of life is 10/1.

2. To receive the Point of Creation for the second half of your life, add the Ruling Energy from the second half of your life to your Emotional Core.

Example continued:

For the second half of life, the RE was 19/10/1. So we'll take 1 and add it to the last number of the EC, 1.

1 + 1 = 2

So, the PoC for the second half of life is 2.

Vortex

The vortex consists of 3 numbers that are represented by the final number in the Emotional Core, Ruling Energy, and Point of Creation. These are your most predominant energies, and they are the medium through which you understand the energetic dynamic that is present in your relationships.

Example: *Birthday – 3/15/1954*

EC = 28/10/1

RE = 9, 19/10/1

PoC = 10/1, 2

For the first half of life, the vortex is 1/9/1.

For the second half, it is 1/1/2.

To discover the dynamic that two people have in a relationship, you would first have to identify what each of their vortices are, which we'll go into further in the chapters on Relationships and the corresponding section for your numbers.

Further Examples

Since it is so important to understand how to calculate the EC, RE and PoC, as well as to identify the vortices for a life, we've included a few more examples using different birth dates so that you can follow along with the calculations and make sure they make sense to you.

Once you know your numbers, you'll want to refer to the corresponding topic in this book to understand their significance and how they apply to you.

Birth date: 12/8/1992

EC = 32/5   **1 + 2 + 8 + 1 + 9 + 9 + 2 = 32**
3 + 2 = 5

RE = 11/2 (1st half)   **1 + 2 + 8 = 11**
1 + 1 = 2

RE = 21/3 (2nd half)   **1 + 9 + 9 + 2 = 21**
2 + 1 = 3

PoC = 7 (1st half)   **5 + 2 = 7**

PoC = 8 (2nd half)   **5 + 3 = 8**

Vortex (1st half)
EC = 5
RE = 2
PoC = 7

Vortex (2nd half)
EC = 5
RE = 3
PoC = 8

Birth date: 2/3/2000

EC = 7 **2 + 3 + 2 + 0 + 0 + 0 = 7**

RE = 5 (1st half) **2 + 3 = 5**

RE = 2 (2nd half) **2 + 0 + 0 + 0 = 2**

PoC = 12/3 (1st half) **7 + 5 = 12**
1 + 2 = 3

PoC = 9 (2nd half) **7 + 2 = 9**

Vortex (1st half)
EC = 7
RE = 5
PoC = 3

Vortex (2nd half)
EC = 7
RE = 2
PoC = 9

Discovering Your Self

Emotional Core

4 - Stability and Process
Those that posses a 4 deal with the daily challenge of creating an identity for themselves in which they feel comfortable and accepted by others.

This number has a strong sense imagery both on the interior and exterior. Because of this, they are always aware of society-based descriptions such as image, label, value, race, sexuality and status.

They also have the tendency to be very judgmental at certain times, but not always in a negative way.

These individuals have great ideas that fit into society's ideas of success, but they often skip steps that they would need to take in order to reach optimal success, a success that is continuously expanding. Creating patience and realizing that all great ideas take time, a continuous work ethic and a drive to carry it out is extremely helpful in developing the process.

In the end it is extremely important for these individuals to find positive ways to see themselves and others, while continuing to be patient in every moment.

5 - Freedom and Discipline
Fives posses a great ability to create experiences that are inclusive of others, using their intuition to feel out a way to create an experience that will be enjoyable for everybody involved. Because they have this

ability, they always want to help others, especially people that are close to them.

These individuals are incredibly gifted in multiple arenas. This group of people also prospers in anything that they set their minds to. Because of this, they have a tendency to get bored very easily, as nothing seems challenging enough for them. As a result, their biggest challenge is to discover their true passion, while developing discipline to reach their highest potential. This can result in over-discipline, and it also leads them to suppress their natural desires to engage in new experiences.

It is extremely important for 5s to find consistent ways to balance their need for discipline while finding different ways to enjoy their everyday lives.

6 – Vision and Acceptance

Because they have an incredible ability to visualize the perfect outcome, these individuals tend to see every moment of their lives as not quite good enough.

On the other side, when they learn that there is no completely perfect moment, they find that it is much easier to enjoy the positives of every experience.

These abilities also extend into themselves and into others by providing them with a strong sense of their individual values and flaws, as well as other people's. This may put them into situations where they feel entitled to criticize others. By doing this, they either come off as complainers or motivators, depending on whether or not they want to look at the positive or negative side of the circumstance.

These perfection-based images force them to have issues with their own value and self-worth. This issue can become negative if they feel that other people are more valuable than they are. When this occurs they tend to be over-critical in order to place them into a jaded light.

Being able to harness this emotion while viewing other talents as tools can help them to improve their own worth collectively, and this can lead them to a more consistent and positive reality.

7 - Trust and Openness

As the highest sensitive number, 7s possess an intuitiveness toward what the future may hold for them and others in any given situation. This ability causes them to have issues with trust.

As a result, it leads them through periods of life in which they trust their intuition enough to trust others. Then, when it happens to backfire on them, they find it difficult to trust themselves and others again.

Because they have so much knowledge, many perceive them as being know-it-alls, holding their own opinions and thoughts as fact without looking at the greater picture. The greatest downfall of 7s is that they fear abandonment. They usually bring this into their reality because they subconsciously choose scenarios that test their ability to trust.

Their insecurities lead them to feel as if they are being left out many times and, because of this, they constantly require reassurance they are still involved in whatever their communities or groups.

Sevens must recognize that they must cultivate trust inside of themselves first and foremost before they can really spread their wings and fulfill their highest potential.

8 – Abundance and Recognition

Eight is the strongest imagery number and, because of this, people with this number are naturally able to identify their roles and other people's roles within the framework of society. This ability tends to make them very concerned with money, self-image, and levels of success. This leads them to have extreme issues with power and control. They can blatantly overpower and over-control every situation as a direct result of their internal desires to be noticed.

On the other side of this, they can give their power away and be controlled by others when they receive recognition from a person or group of people that they interpret as being valuable.

The most important thing for 8s to realize is that they're naturally going to draw abundance to them.

It is important for this group of people to work with others. They must realize that they will be recognized even more if they can collaborate in a balanced situation without taking control or giving their power away. This can lead them to a place of truly understanding the value that they have always wanted.

9 – Wisdom and Integrity

Being hybrids of feeling and imagery, 9s are faced with challenges like no other. Due to the fact that the greatest way to gain wisdom in this world is through experience, these individuals have more amplified dramatic and traumatic experiences, especially early on in their lives.

They tend to be very stubborn because they possess an inner belief that their idea of how life should be perceived is the most correct.

These individuals have a strong sense of feeling other people's emotions, similar to 3s. The difference is that they also have the critical visualizations of the number 6. Because of this, when the two of these (empathy and visualization) are mixed together, their ability to feel criticism from others as well as toward others is amplified to the extreme.

The most important thing for 9s to be aware of is the discovery of their personal lessons within each and every experience. The more they can learn and then apply to their lives in the future, the easier it will become.

10/1 – Creative Inner Gift with Confidence

Individuals who enjoy the gift of this combination of numbers are given an opportunity to discover their personal inner gifts and build their highest levels of confidence through it. Although zero does posses some of its own traits, it is best described as a number that enhances the numbers that surround it.

In this case, because the zero is in between 1, individuals carrying these numbers are given the chance to have a higher level of creativity than those that carry 1 by itself or even doubled.

Zero signifies that the individual has a predetermined exceptional ability that they must discover. Creating confidence drives these individuals to have easier and more relaxing day-to-day lives.

It is important for people with this number to allow themselves to channel their creativity, through whichever mediums they are passionate about. When this occurs these individuals will be able to expand into their inner gifts.

11/2 - Double Creativity with Confident Balance

Pairing double creative energy with the necessity to find balance can be a rocky road to the promised land. Having inflated issues when it comes to confidence can lead to major issues in the arena of cooperation.

With an amplified sex drive and a competitive edge, these individuals desire activity on a physically and mentally challenging level on a daily basis.

By adding to that an ability to see and feel how individuals get to cooperate with them, their ability to manipulate becomes amplified. This is because their creative energy wants to be released through their daily experiences with others.

On the other hand, people who carry these numbers can be affected in the opposite way, as a lack of confidence leads to over-cooperation. It is important for individuals who are dealing with this group of numbers to creative positive situations that will bring them balance through all facets of their daily lives.

12/3 - Creative Organization with Balanced Expression

Finding outlets to channel their creativity through a balanced life brings these individuals to their highest levels of confidence. In this high state of confidence, they are able to release all doubt and express themselves freely.

Reaching this peak is much easier said than done. These individuals tend to speak and make commitments to themselves and others with which they don't always follow through. It's not that they didn't necessarily have the intention of following through, but their actions don't always align with their intentions.

These individuals are very sensitive in a way that allows them to get others to cooperate with them easily. They are also able to help others in productive ways because they are able to sense exactly what somebody needs in the appropriate moment.

On the other hand, they can also have a hard time cooperating, while attacking others verbally in hurtful ways.

It is immensely important for these individuals to be very aware of how they project their opinions onto others. They must focus on releasing their expressive energy in positive and productive ways. This will help them discover creative balance while achieving high levels of success in their lives.

13/4 - Creative Sensitivity with Expressive Process

Those that have the pleasure of possessing these numbers must find stability within their daily lives, while also finding creative and confident ways to release their expression.

Having a 3 and a 4 next to one another gives these individuals a strong ability to feel and see how others interpret different societal standards. Because of this, they usually have issues with their inner confidence, and they also tend to harbor a lot of doubt.

All of this is reflective of their need to establish stability through their self-image, while reaching a level of acceptance within society where they feel confident and comfortable. It is most important to build a personal foundation that brings them a sense of comfort. This will help them build confidence while releasing their expression constructively in the long run.

14/5 – Creative Process with Stable Freedom

With this combination of numbers, creativity is brought to the table in conjunction with a strong understanding of what it means to be in a process. This leads to an ability to create constructive, disciplined experiences.

Fives are usually experience junkies, and they naturally enjoy being a part of group activities that allow them to share their freedom with others. By mixing this with the ability to create a stable foundation that allows them to build confidence in themselves, they are able to reach massive goals. This manifests as reaching significant levels within society because others see that these individuals have a natural ability to understand the process that leads to a common goal using constructive group discipline.

For these individuals, not getting ahead of themselves and overcoming the boredom that they feel with the everyday process will help them to find their deep need to feel free in the long run.

15/6 – Creative Freedom with Disciplined Acceptance

With this combination of receptive numbers together, carriers of a 15/6 have the ability to sense how to organize groups of people in a very creative way.

On the other hand, if they do not have structure and they lack discipline, they tend to lose confidence in what they're trying to achieve. These individuals have a tendency to be addicts, as 1s influence substance abuse and 5s are associated with being experience junkies.

Many times they set expectations for themselves and, when those expectations are not met, they are disappointed. This leads them to feel that no moment is ever perfect, and they are always striving for something better.

When this group of people gets negative or out of balance, it has the potential to lead to major struggles in their daily lives, especially in relation to their closest relationships. On the positive side, if these individuals can discipline themselves on a daily basis, they have more confidence when they are able to get out and enjoy their freedom.

It is imperative for them to focus on the good things that come out of every moment that they experience while staying away from setting expectations.

16/7 - Creative Vision with Intuitive Trust

Out of instinct, these individuals have intense creativity and imagery that is based on structure. Matching this with the intuitiveness that a 7 has, they will possess high levels of knowledge about what needs to be accomplished in order for them to achieve any sort of goal.

One of the biggest issues for these individuals will be finding ways to continue with endeavors long-term. Although they have great ideas and wish to follow through with them, when bumps in the road arise, 6s tend to stop trying because if they never put any effort forth in the first place, they have never actually failed.

It is important to acknowledge the mixture of abandonment with 1's lack of desire to compete. With this dynamic, these individuals may find that they never truly exert all of themselves in anything that they do.

On the other hand, if they are able to accept that there will be changes along the journey and are able to trust that they are on the right track, they will find more confidence in the everyday process that will lead them to achieving their goals.

17/8 – Confident Trust with Intuitive Abundance

This is one of the few number combinations that will naturally thrive within our society if they can find confidence within their intuitiveness.

Blending 1 and 7 together creates a hybrid of creativity and intuition, which gives these people an incredible ability to create outcomes for themselves that they subconsciously know others will be happy with. Extending this into their need to be recognized leads them to find themselves in prevalent roles within our society when they have both confidence and trust in themselves.

On the other hand, these individuals will constantly struggle with trust issues and lack of confidence. They'll tend to find relationships that make them feel recognized but in which they can keep the upper hand in order to be the one to abandon the other person before they can be abandoned.

At times they can be very manipulative in order to have control and power over situations within their lives. This comes from their need to be recognized and their intuitive nature that allows them to know exactly what to say in order to get others to do what they please. This can also be affected by the 1 because they feel inferior if they lose.

When 8s have the ability to get others to agree with them, it provides them with a sense of confidence. Ultimately, these individuals must focus on constructive ways in which they can release their creativity through their trust in order to cultivate confidence and recognition.

18/9 - Creative Recognition with Inherent Wisdom

Blending both confidence and recognition together can create an incredibly powerful mind that is capable of accomplishing almost anything it attempts.

On the other hand, they can come off as very arrogant, superficial, and confrontational. This part of them will be amplified by the 9, which will lead them into a number of challenging experiences that will give them the wisdom to correct these characteristics.

On the positive side of things, having 9 as their last number gives them an opportunity to mature faster than others, and if they can do this in a positive manner, their potential is endless.

By instilling confidence in themselves at a young age and by learning from every experience, abundance will manifest itself in all different areas of life. Because of this, it is extremely important not to allow their tempers to get the best of them, while looking at every experience as a test to learn and grow.

19/10/1 - Confident Wisdom with Creative Inner Gift and Confidence

Having three 1s makes these individuals incredibly unique. Adding 0 and 9 into the mix only elevates these people to massive change and discovery through their daily life experiences that will allow them to gain lessons.

Since 9 lies within the first two numbers, early on in these individuals' lives they will experience many amplified events that will give them the opportunity to learn and grow. The biggest issue will be their level of confidence that leads them to repeating the same mistakes over and over again.

With the 9 present, each of these individuals possesses a special, unique inner gift. The sooner they can reveal this gift and focus their time and energy onto it, the more productive and confident they will be with themselves.

Most importantly, these people need to discover the most positive and constructive ways to release their creativity on a daily basis. If this does not occur it can lead to many lost opportunities and even heartache.

20/2 – Cooperative Inner Gift with Balance

The combination of 0 with any number is truly unique, and in this situation it gives the opportunity to enhance these individuals' abilities to create cooperation in whatever realm that is best suited for them.

On the other hand, these people are going to have many issues with their ability to cooperate with others, which will often lead to resentful outcomes, either toward themselves or toward others.

It is important for them to understand that their abilities to create structure and to organize and plan can be utilized to its highest potential if they are able to work with others and find balance within those relationships.

Balance is the key to all of the issues that go on within their daily lives. They must not over-give or over-take, but finding clarity and balance between them will enhance their inner gifts and it will eventually lead them to have more joyful daily experiences.

21/3 – Balanced Creativity with Sensitive Expression

These numbers will be channeled in a positive way by productively organizing creative outlets for expression. These individuals often complain about being off-balanced while blaming this on their environments and using it as a justification to engage in addictive behaviors.

These individuals are also very sensitive to other people and their energies, and as a result, they commonly find themselves at the mercy of other people and their demands.

They have the tendency to engage in unproductive and manipulative behaviors. What drives them to end up in these situations is that they are frequently in search of a fairy tale experience, and when this is not presented to them, they turn to tragedy.

These individuals must understand that life is what they make of it, and when they come to this realization, they will harness their inner creativity and strong abilities to express themselves.

22/4 - Double Cooperative Balance with Stabilizing Process

With the duplication of the number 2, those that carry these numbers have an incredible ability to create cooperative situations inside of themselves and with others in their lives.

Their biggest challenge is balancing how much they give and take from others, which will directly predict the amount of personal resentment and stress that they feel.

How well they balance themselves will determine their level of stability and patience within their lives. When they are out of balance they are easily irritated and impatient with those around them while anticipating each moment.

On the other hand, when they find balance in all facets of their lives they are able to access patience, while also finding a step-by-step daily routine that includes other people in the process of achieving a collective goal.

23/5 - Balanced Expression with Disciplined Freedom

One of the most unique groups of people out there, these individuals have distinct strengths in their abilities to sense what others enjoy while also balancing their expression and discipline.

Due to their desire to help others and the sensitivity that they have to sympathize with others, these people tend to put themselves in relationships in which they over-cooperate. When this occurs, they end up feeling resentment if they don't receive what they had hoped for in return.

Although most people deal with these issues, 2s tend to dwell on it more than your average person. This is because they suppress their expression, holding in their true feelings until they finally release them all in any given moment.

It's essential for these individuals to create balance in how much they give and how much they take. They must understand that it is a great thing to be able to help others, but in the meantime, they still need to be aware of how much they're taking away from themselves. It is important that they work on themselves and give to themselves before they focus on helping other people.

24/6 - Cooperative Process with Stable Acceptance

24/6s have a strong ability to succeed within the frameworks of our society if they don't discover alternative routes.

With 2's ability to get others to cooperate with them, mixed directly with the foundation-building 4, they can create nearly flawless plans through the energy of a 6.

No matter what the situation is, these individuals are great at organizing and are very idealistic, but their patience is continuously tested, and many times they find themselves doing way too much for others while failing to receive what they had expected in return.

They also have issues with over-criticizing themselves and others. This has the potential to affect them and the people that surround them with significantly. This is because they begin to over-cooperate, which leads them to find themselves in settings where they become impatient. They become critical and resentful when situations don't turn out the way they had expected.

This group of people can fall into periods in which they do not care about anything that has to do with success and personal growth. This is because 6s have issues with self-worth. They believe that if they never truly try they will never have to experience failure. As a result, they find stability in whatever doesn't challenge them. At the same time they want to find a way to succeed and feel more value.

They must realize that they will only grow and expand when they step outside of their comfort zones, which means taking on challenges.

Ultimately, it is important for these individuals to accept themselves and others for who they are while finding ways to constructively work and improve through a step-by-step process.

25/7 - Balanced Discipline with Trusted Openness

This combination of numbers is enormously intuitive, with the ability to be very receptive to other people and their energies.

In addition to this, these individuals are very gifted physically, whether it be athletically or in relation to their physical appearances.

Fives have a desire to always help others and, because of this, this number tends to find themselves over-cooperating with others. This can lead them to being taken advantage of, leaving them with a feeling of resentment toward whomever benefited from their cooperation.

This may also reflect their fear of abandonment, which is influenced by the number 7, and can get them in situations in which they are constantly in a state of giving while at the same time feeling as if at any moment they are going to be left out of the loop.

On the other hand, this individual has an incredible sense of how to get others to not only trust them but also cooperate with them. Their sense of freedom allows them to create environments from which communities can find enjoyment and benefit. They have an incredible ability to work with others and be in leadership roles.

It is most important for them to find ways in which they can balance their discipline throughout their daily lives, because 5s tend to get bored very easily.

In addition, this group of people has the potential to develop some very destructive habits if they're not aware and very careful. When it comes down to it, their personal discipline will directly affect the trust that they have in themselves and others. When they possess inner-trust they can reflect this in their relationships, and they can be very positive people within their communities that others can depend on.

26/8 – Cooperative Vision with Abundant Recognition

This group of people has an incredible ability to visualize perfection that aligns with society's expectations of success. They are also able to create this level of success with other people.

Through the cooperation of 2 and the vision of 6, these individuals are able to find ways to be recognized in high social standards. These are standards that they're capable of reaching no matter where they are along their journey.

What tends to be the issue here is that 6 causes them to set high expectations for themselves, and when it doesn't turn out the way it was planned there are two reactions. The first is a submissive "I don't care" attitude in which they receive recognition because they are upset about something. The second reaction is when they lash out vocally until they get someone or something to cooperate with them. They do this in order for to feel recognized.

It is extremely important for 26/8s to find balance in their amount of control and power that they possess over others. They may at times come off as bossy and very critical of the people that surround them.

Focusing on accepting themselves and others for who they are and finding daily balance within their everyday relationships will lead them to naturally abundant realities.

27/9 – Balanced Openness with Trusted Wisdom

The ability to intuitively feel how others are thinking and feeling can give this group of people a deep understanding of others' perceptions and interpretations of everyday life and the present moment.

On the other side, they can get lost in interpreting what they are reading from others. This has the potential to lead them to fear of abandonment and, because of this, they over-cooperate with others.

Due to the 9 that is present, all of their experiences will be amplified. As a result, the tendency to put themselves in relationships in which they are able to do the abandoning first reflects how much they really trust themselves.

On the other hand, they can cooperate with somebody or a group of people too much. They do this until fear creates resentment, then they create a situation for them to be abandoned.

These people tend to carry a very high level of intuitive wisdom that derives from the influences that surround their lives and the personal lessons they have gained through their own experiences. It is very important for these individuals to focus on learning from their experiences and not repeating the same mistakes. In the long run, this is what will build trust in their intuitive wisdom.

28/10/1 – Cooperative Recognition with Creative Inner Gift and Confidence

Recognition is the root of these individuals' ability to live within a confident reality. Finding balance when it comes to cooperation and control of the present moment is the biggest challenge for them.

When these individuals over-cooperate, it is usually a reaction to their lack of recognition from others that reflects a lack of confidence from within.

What can also happen is that they will create recognition for themselves, by getting other people to cooperate by manipulating them or going on a power trip. This leads them to be more confident, but they also become difficult to be around because they are always micromanaging others.

These individuals can be great leaders if they constructively discover ways in which they can access their inner gifts and use them to fulfill their internal desires to be recognized. This can bring them to their highest levels of personal productivity and confidence.

It is also important for these individuals to zoom out and take a look at the larger picture, while ceasing to worry about being better than others. Life will be much simpler when this occurs, and it will also inevitably bring them positive recognition, which will bring out the purest form of confidence within.

29/11/2 – Balanced Integrity with Amplified Creative Confidence and Cooperation

Extremely gifted in the realms of cooperation, these individuals tend to be very deceptive when it comes to working with others.

Since they possess such wisdom and integrity that derives from the 9, they find it very easy to push their way of life onto others whether it may be positive or negative. They tend to expand this in their creativity, which is where they naturally find ways to create cooperation in one form or another.

The challenge for these individuals is to find a balance between influencing others and pushing their beliefs or ways of life onto others. Many times they are perceived as being very manipulative, and the more they manipulate in negative ways, the worse they feel about themselves. Although this may not always be obvious to the observer, it is very present at their cores.

On the other hand, when these individuals use this ability in a positive way, they can be powerful leaders and teammates. Because of their enhanced ability to get others to cooperate with them, they have a strong and determined sense of how to work well with others. With this, they can take the initiative to lead through their expanded wisdom and confidence.

It is important for these people to focus on constructive ways to release their creativity. This will present situations in which they will act as leaders rather than manipulators.

30/3 – Expressive Inner Gift with Sensitivity

These people find themselves with incredible gifts when it comes to expression and sensitivity due to a heightened sense of others' emotions.

By itself, 3 allows the individual to interpret how the emotions of other people are running just by looking at them and reading their body language. This can be both a strength and a weakness.

On the strong side of it, they can feel what needs to be said within their comfort zone. Normally in small groups or one-on-one situations they can be great listeners for people to come to when advice is needed.

On the weak side, they can use that sense to create deception for others normally in the form of manipulation.

All of which reflects the doubt that they hold within, leading them to deceive others into thinking that all is well while inside they're a giant ball of mixed emotions.

It is extremely important for these individuals to find positive and constructive ways to release their expression. In the end this will lead them to truly discover what their inner gift is and apply it to this world in many different forms.

31/4 – Sensitive Creativity with Confident Stability

By possessing sensitivity mixed with a creative sense of social-based imagery, this group of people is incredibly gifted in the realms of how to succeed within the current structure of our society.

They have a strong desire to create personal stability and this directly reflects in their confidence-levels and the levels of doubt that they hold.

At times these individuals find themselves so caught up in the need for a stable identity that they overlook the true value of their relationships with others. Rather than associating with certain people because they enjoy their company, they choose to spend time with individuals who they believe hold higher social status.

These individuals also tend to find small social groups that fit their particular image of themselves, which gives them a sense of comfort.

Confidence dictates success in everyday moments for these individuals. It is extremely important to be aware of the fact that confidence is found within and is not created outwardly.

With this said, relying on others to provide this group of people with confidence creates self-doubt, which is amplified due to the 3 that is present here.

Ultimately, it is important for them to find productive ways to release their expression and creativity on a daily basis. When these individuals can find productive ways to regularly release their expression and creativity and they are able to tie this in with a profession, the opportunities are endless to have a stable, thriving reality.

32/5 - Expressive Balance with Cooperative Freedom

The combination of expressive sensitivity into cooperative balance allows carriers of these numbers to have a strong understanding of how to organize themselves and extend that organization to others. This directly correlates with their ability to feel out the energetic needs of an environment.

These individuals tend to struggle with a desire to help others too much, which can cause a lot of stress for them when the people that they reach out to don't necessarily appreciate or learn from whatever 32/5s have to offer.

This can create great amounts of resentment, and this contributes to the doubt that they feel about themselves and others. It is important for them to balance out their sensitivity for others with exactly what and how much they offer to others. It is imperative for them to be aware of when people are taking advantage of them, while taking steps to make sure that it doesn't happen to them in the first place.

On the other hand, these individuals are always a joy to be around, and can always find fun in any situation.

They have the potential to get bored with life and, therefore, it is important for them to have variety within their lives by discovering many different passions and outlets of expression.

When 32/5s discover their passion through discipline while navigating their boredom productively, this will bring them to their highest level of freedom. It is important, however, for them to remember that balance is the key for their success.

33/6 – Double Expressive Sensitivity with Visual Acceptance

These individuals are immensely strong and sensitive to the world around them.

This group of people possess a unique ability to feel other people's emotions, while placing individuals in different categories of value. The 6 is very focused on perfection, and the 3 instills doubt inside of 33/6s. With this combination, they find themselves complaining a great deal.

It is important for these individuals to focus on creating positive outcomes for themselves. This can be approached through the realization that no moment is ever perfect, while finding ways to accept that there are flaws in each and every one of us. Rather than using their instincts to criticize negatively, they have the ability to flip this around and become somebody that motivates themselves and others through their positive traits.

Something else to be wary of is that 6s tend to be very self-destructive, because they start to live as if they can't fail if they never try. Living through this framework can create an immense amount of blocked expression and doubt that has the potential to hold them back from living in a positive light.

Challenging themselves to balance the urges that can manifest as self-destructive and blocked expression will ultimately be much more productive for them in the future. This will create a more positive reality for themselves and all those that surround them.

34/7 - Expressive Stability with Trusted Process

These individuals have the ability to both feel the emotions of other people and what they are going through, while also being able to relate to others very deeply through their own identity that they have created for themselves.

What brings transcendence to carriers of these numbers is the intuitiveness that leads them to build foundation with ease. This leaves them with a sense of understanding and appreciating their purpose here on Earth.

34/7s struggle with their ability to create stability in their personal lives, while also having good intentions in pursuing their passions. Because of the 7 that is present, these individuals present themselves as if they know everything, while in the meantime, they do not fully-grasp and comprehend the truth of what they are presenting.

This tendency is influenced by the 4 that wants to be admired by others. The biggest challenge here is to overcome their self-doubt, while taking the time to process each step along any path they wish to take.

With 7's intuition and 4's tendency to rush, it can negatively affect these individuals when they do not allow themselves to clearly understand that everything takes time and patience to develop. Overall, when these individuals can trust themselves and the steps that are needed to have a successful journey, the outcome will inevitably be growth.

35/8 – Expressive Discipline with Abundant Recognition

This combination of numbers creates abundance in its most expressive form. Individuals experiencing this energy deal with a natural tendency to be recognized, which usually comes in the form of freedom or discipline situations. When they are able to identify their strongest attributes toward our world, they are able to find comfort in the amount of recognition that they receive.

Developing discipline through their boredom that is created by the number 5, they can build an identity everybody admires, giving them an abundance of freedom.

35/8s can often be the most abundant human beings because of their ability to feel that numbers 3, 5, and 8 provide. Their ability to sense feelings from others while promoting positive outlets to express their freedom makes them favorites of the crowd.

This is very rewarding for 35/8s, but when their intentions are not to gain recognition, they learn that abundance naturally comes to them when they are humble.

36/9 - Expressive Vision with Valued Integrity

Strong-willed and aggressive while subtle at the same time, these individuals have an incredible sense of our social and economic world.

Being driven through the number 9 creates a lot of experiences that challenge these individuals to build their own integrity. That is driven through the value that correlates with 6 and the sensitivity that correlates with 3. This combination behind the number 9 tends to bring this group of people into self-destructive behaviors that are caused by the 6 and amplified by the 9.

All of this reflects into the 3's fairy tale or tragedy outlook on life. Criticism, along with hypocritical actions tend to be the main reflection for these humans when they find themselves in negative situations.

The biggest challenge here is to be able to accept the level of value they are currently in, while being able to visualize the best path forward in order to improve their lives. Focusing on taking real action rather than just talking about it can help these humans immensely when it comes to making productive changes.

Overall, when 36/9s can harness themselves to a project that is aligned with a higher integrity for the greater good of all, they will find themselves and their personal well-being at its highest.

37/10/1 - Expressive Trust with Creative Inner Gift and Confidence

Emotionally driven, this person's ability to feel and anticipate the moments as they come is exponential. This strength can many times backfire when there is a lack of confidence, which causes a feeling of lost trust and doubt.

The fear of the unknown challenges the carriers of these numbers as well. When they are able to access their inherent gifts and apply them, their confidence expands. When this occurs they can replace the doubt with expanded intuition, creating an incredible reality for themselves.

They must understand the importance of revealing their inner gift, as it will enable a higher level of trust inside of themselves in relation to others, and in relation to their ultimate fates.

For example, you can think of it as working backward starting from 0. Finding their true passion will allow the 1 to find self-confidence, which leads to creativity inside of their passion.

In addition, the 7 will open up trust with themselves and others. It will also provide the teaching that, ultimately, we have no control over our divine life paths, and that it is very important to be present and live in each moment with no future expectations.

After the 1 and 7 have become balanced, the 3 will remove any type of self-doubt, allowing these people to be fully expressive in each and every situation in which they may have held in emotions in the past.

38/11/2 - Expressive Recognition with Balanced Creativity and Confident Cooperation

Individuals who carry these numbers have the most energetically gifted minds, as these individuals are able to structure their creativity in a way that draws abundance toward them. The challenge for these individuals is whether they harness this energy in a positive or negative way.

These individuals cooperate with others with ease, and this can frequently be challenging for them. When they are able to find productive ways to funnel their creativity, they work very well in groups and on teams.

On the other hand, when their creativity is controlled by others, their desire for recognition often pushes them to lash out because they want to be recognized.

In other circumstances they also have a tendency to be over-cooperative, which leads them to resentment. This forces them into a vibration that is less confident, controversial, and creatively blocked. Many times this manifests itself into feelings of resentment, addiction, or a strong desire to control others.

When these individuals can find a sense of confidence by harnessing patience and acceptance of who they are becoming they will feel less doubt about themselves and others while also being much more constructive and organized with their time.

39/12/3 - Expressive Wisdom with Confident Balance and Sensitivity

This is an extreme version of expressive energy especially since it is connected with 9, 1, and 2.

Having 3 as the main emotional number is a test within itself, but to add the amplified experiences of 9 with the unsettledness of 1 and the ability to get others to cooperate of 2 can leave these people in a whirlwind of change and uncertainty.

Challenged all the time with feeling that they're living either a fairy tale or tragedy this tends to reflect through 9 making every experience just a bit more extreme.

It's important for these individuals to understand that they are naturally here to build integrity in themselves while also being able to harness both expressive and creative energy properly.

When they find themselves out of balance they, more often than not, will find themselves constantly complaining, engaging in addictive behaviors, and coming off as hypocrites. For these humans to harness a better sense of who they are it is important that they find lessons through everything that goes on in their current moments and all that has occurred throughout their life thus far.

Through this they can begin to put their best foot forward and build a deeper sense of confidence and positive expression.

40/4 – Stable Inner Gift with Process

This emotional combination is not only unique because it possesses a 0, but also because it is surrounded by the number 4.

Being able to manifest an inner gift inside of the structural foundation of a personal identity can bring some very rare abilities into this world. The biggest challenge for 40/4s is harnessing patience inside of themselves in order to find their true gifts, while being able to manifest this through a steady process.

This group of people will be over-dramatic at times, putting themselves in positions where they receive judgment from others. This has the potential to negatively affect those individuals who have low self-worth.

When this energy is harnessed, these individuals are able to build themselves as leaders that others in society will look up to and strive to be. This can be achieved by focusing on the current tasks in their environments that will bring them along to the next step in their journeys.

Recognizing that the true joy in life is in seeing our dreams come to life while experiencing each step along the way will make the flow of life graceful and effortless.

41/5 – Stable Confidence with Creative Freedom

Creating a foundation with confidence has the potential to produce a very interesting journey through the balance of freedom and discipline. When these individuals are able to embrace a healthy balance of freedom and discipline, they are able to harness extremely high confidence in their abilities and personal identities.

The challenge for these individuals is finding that balance, while identifying when this balance is off. When they are too relaxed, the 1 will dive into more addictive behaviors while lacking responsibility and patience with their lives. When they have too much discipline, these individuals might find themselves very frustrated with a lack of variety in their lives, while never truly finding happiness within the persona that they have build throughout their process.

Although they find themselves in many different extremes throughout their lives, when they can take responsibility for their actions and understand that they naturally need to create both freedom and discipline, they are able to manifest their full potential.

42/6 – Stable Balance with Cooperative Vision

Combining the sharp, perfection-based energy of a 6 with the organizational skills that a 2 possesses, these individuals use this energy in order to manifest an identity for themselves.

They can have issues with their self-worth as well as the direction and process that they wish to see their lives take. This can lead them to rely on others as a result of the 2's ability to render cooperation from others.

When they are in a more productive mindset they can be very patient with the steps that are needed to complete a goal or receive high praise from their peers.

When they are unproductive, they tend to find themselves misled and self-destructive. They start to believe that if they never really try, then they have never actually failed in accomplishing their dreams.

When these individuals can visualize the steps that are needed to complete their process while organizing themselves to execute each step, they will always achieve success.

43/7 – Stable Expression with Sensitive Trust

With a unique ability to pick up on the emotions of other people using their intuition, these individuals have a great sense of how to gain the trust of other people while presenting an image of themselves. What has the potential to be an issue here is whether they're building a positive or negative image for themselves.

Because they feel the need to find productive arenas that will allow them to express how they feel, they will often open up too much in a one-on-one setting, while being over-dramatic and complaining. In addition, because 3s look at life as a fairy tale or tragedy, 43/7s can find themselves falling in love way too quickly, and then when they are abandoned, they look at it as the biggest tragedy of their lives.

In addition, they find themselves creating the persona of knowing it all when they get side-tracked from the steps that need to be taken in order to create any task.

When these individuals can focus on the process of their lives while also using their intuition and self-expression positively, they have the potential to be powerful and influential contributors to any team while also living a much smoother lifestyle.

44/8 - Double Stability with Processed Abundance

These individuals have an uncanny ability to manifest a very recognizable image for themselves. What is up in the air is whether they manifest this image positively or negatively. When they find themselves ahead of the process, they tend to be overpowering while presenting an insecure picture of themselves to others.

Fours usually have a thrill for drama and, because of this, these individuals tend to create a lot of opportunities for others to recognize them even in the most simple forms.

They have strong foundational minds, and these individuals can find themselves easily attached to a particular role or identity within their lives that they feel most comfortable portraying.

When these individuals can understand that natural recognition will come to them if they are patient with whatever they put their energy into, this will inevitably lead to an outcome of abundance.

45/9 - Stable Freedom with Disciplined Integrity

These individuals are constantly tested with their ability to harness the freedom and discipline that is associated with the number 5, in addition to the amplified changes and experiences that 9 presents. This leaves these individuals with the challenge of establishing any type of productive identities for themselves.

These individuals are very stubborn due to the personal integrity of 9. They also have a difficult time recognizing whether or not they're too free or too disciplined. This can get them into a number of bad habits, manifesting as impatience with life and where they currently stand.

When carriers of 45/9 find balance and discover lessons from their past, this can help them grow and begin to establish themselves as well-respected.

It is of the utmost importance for these people not to find dependence on others but rather to embrace their independence and understand that taking responsibility for their own actions puts their best foot forward.

46/10/1 – Stable Vision with Creative Gift and Confidence

This individual is a very unique human, as only 13 birthdays allow them to reach this Emotional Core.

Blending 4 and 6 together mixed with the creativity of 1 creates a wild and unique mind. These individuals usually have lower self-confidence, which leads them to engage in addictive and destructive behaviors.

For these individuals, it is important to establish a creative process that will encompass the steps that they will take in order to reach their peaks. They must visualize this process, and when this journey is embarked on they have taken the first step in getting their mind on the right track.

Another obstacle for these individuals is discovering their inherent gifts that can be identified by the 0. They must understand that this will not always come easily, and that there will most certainly be a process.

It is also important for them to realize that goals that are set but aren't reached are learning opportunities. When these individuals accept what is and cultivate a competitive drive, they are fueled to reach the pinnacle of life that they have always desired.

47/11/2 – Stable Intuition with Double Confidence and Creative Balance

This combination of numbers is extremely rare, as there are only 5 days that could reach this high combination together.

What makes this combination especially interesting is that there is a set of two 1s together and they are paired with a 7. Together, these numbers are a potent combination, but it can be very challenging to manifest positively with this energetic makeup.

When these individuals find themselves over-compensating for others because of the 2, they lose confidence in themselves. This results in addictive behaviors, impatience, or resistance to being productive in any sense.

On the other side of that, if they are able to harness this energy in a productive way, they are capable of being extremely resourceful, understanding how to balance those around them through their intuition, strong way with words, and ability to identify others' strengths and weaknesses.

Before they are able to get to this proficiency level, they must establish a process, and from there they must trust that they can create the organization to execute the task at hand.

The sooner these individuals realize how truly special they are, the sooner their lives can begin to take off.

48/12/3 - Stable Abundance with Creative Balance and Cooperative Expression

9/29/1999 is the only day for the next 900-odd years until we have a human like this presented to us on this Earth.

This extremely rare person will hold the task of harnessing how to organize a creative expression that brings them a recognizable identity that they're happy with.

When in harmony, these individuals will have the ability to do great things due to their rare blend of emotions.

However, if they don't curb the urge to rush the process and their concerns about not holding the highest level of recognition, these individuals could find themselves in predicaments that create addictive behaviors, under cooperation with those around them, and a doubt-filled reality where they feel they can't ever find balance.

So for these extremely rare individuals, allow life to come to you and understand that abundance is inevitable the more you keep yourself in a positive light.

Ruling Energy

2 – Cooperation and Balance

Being ruled by a 2 presents many challenges within the execution of daily tasks on an everyday basis.

Organization is huge for these individuals to create a sense of balance in their lives. They will constantly be tested in regard to how much they give and take from others. When this balance is off they will create issues of resentment in their lives.

When they are able to establish a direction in which to take their lives, they will create a healthy balance of giving and receiving while manifesting an ability to manage their time wisely.

Once this has been obtained these individuals can be incredible people to work with in groups and will also have the extensive ability to organize and lead group activities that many people can benefit from.

3 – Expression and Sensitivity

Being ruled by a 3 brings the challenge of finding productive ways to release expression while also remaining aware of the natural tendency to have emotionally-driven experiences.

The most predominant experience that holds these individuals back is the feeling of doubt about the direction in which their lives are headed and the influences that surround them. Life may seem to them like a dichotomy of either being a fairy tale or a tragedy.

It is extremely important for these individuals to realize that they are the only ones that can determine how their lives will proceed.

When the tragedy is created, these individuals will complain about everything that surrounds them by only focusing on the negativity and how it is affecting their well-being. When these individuals do get into the mindset of seeing their lives as tragedies, they will complain about everything that surrounds them by only focusing on the negativity. This significantly affects their well-being.

It is important for them to realize that they have to focus on the positives of life and the changes that they personally need to make in order to follow through.

Once these individuals find productive ways to feel good about themselves, their natural expression can flow smoothly without the creation of any doubt about who they truly are.

4 – Stability and Process

The biggest challenge in being ruled by a 4 is the ability to establish an identity within society with which these individuals feel comfortable. The test here is patience and understanding that there is a process that goes along with every great achievement.

When these individuals find themselves unsure of who they are they can be idealistic and overly-dramatic. In other words, they see the end of the rainbow, but they never actually take accountability for the steps that are necessary to get there.

They can come off as very judgmental, but they can also be placed into situations where they are ridiculed by their peers when they are out of balance. Focusing on themselves rather than how others perceive them is the first step for them to begin creating a foundation for the person that they envision themselves to be.

When these individuals can create a positive direction for themselves and understand that everyday another step needs to be taken in order to achieve the end goal, their potential is limitless.

5 - Freedom and Discipline

These individuals have the ultimate balancing act of trying to find different outlets in which to have fun and enjoy life while also creating a sense of discipline. This is a challenge that will always test these individuals.

When they find themselves struggling it usually reflects in two main attributes, in their dependence on others and their desire to help others around them excessively.

When they have an uncontrolled sense of freedom they find themselves depending on others to take care of their personal needs, and many times this causes them to feel trapped.

The feeling of being trapped can also set in when the mindset of being too disciplined causes them to help others too much. Because of this, they must take on more responsibility while those around them don't put as much effort in but still reap the benefits.

When these individuals are able to establish a sense of balance within these two energies, they will find that life will accommodate them when they establish a greater sense of independence and can act as a role model for others rather than acting as a selfless caregiver.

6 – Vision and Acceptance

Constantly seeking validation for their existence, these individuals can find themselves always trying to do more than what is actually needed from them.

Struggling with self-worth, they may feel that they are never really good enough to meet their parents' expectations.

On the other hand, they may also feel that they have more value than their parents ever could have and that the only thing that is holding them back is their families.

It is important for these individuals to accept the reality that they were born into and make the best out of all situations, rather than pointing out all the reasons why they can't succeed.

Being ruled by a 6 is incredible because their minds are naturally sharp and others around them want to see them reach their highest potential. If this is not the case, 6s can use this energy to fuel themselves to achieve while others tend to send criticism their way, which is a natural experience for 6s.

It is important for them to be aware that at certain times they will find themselves in self-destructive behaviors and that they must learn to minimize them.

Overall, their production and personal value is generated solely with the path that they wish to create for themselves based on how positive or negative they are on a daily basis.

7 – Trust and Openness

A reality that is driven through trust creates a major challenge: abandonment.

Throughout their lives, abandonment will be a huge theme. In their lives they will consistently be abandoned by people that they care about, and they will also abandon others.

As challenging as this may be, all of this abandonment is happening for a reason. It is helping these individuals to harness their intuition and their ability to see what is truly important in life. They will naturally seek a higher purpose, but it is important for them not to get too lost along the spiritual path.

The intuition that 7s possess gives them a deep understanding that there is more to this world than what meets the eye. Because of this, others perceive them as know-it-alls, as well as individuals who never truly find direction.

All of this can lead this group of people to look for reassurance from others that they are in fact important to those that they care about.

Sevens must stick to something and fully trust that if they continue on that particular path, they have the potential to fully open up to who they truly are. They will also have more control of who and what comes in and out of their lives.

8 – Abundance and Recognition

Having an 8 as your ruling number can be both very challenging as well as very profitable when harnessed through patience and recognition of the steps needed to create a prosperous foundation.

What tends to be most apparent in those ruled by 8 is that they are constantly being recognized whether it is positive or negative. Many times they may not even be concerned for others, but they will naturally attract others to them.

They time and time again feel as if they are being overlooked and, therefore, they become either pushy or driven by receiving recognition from others.

When this group of people realizes that positive recognition is driven solely through their actions rather than their words, they begin to find the proper ways to create their ideal processes in their lives. At this point, if they can apply themselves, step-by-step abundance will inevitably come.

9 – Wisdom and Integrity

This energy will create constant tests and changes throughout their lives in order for them to grow and expand their integrity of what this world is really all about.

This group of people may come off to others as wise beyond their years, while at the same time their actions reflect immaturity.

Often those ruled by a 9 will find themselves in hypocritical situations in which they lack responsibility for their actions. When these individuals can start looking at their past and the mistakes they have made as lessons that they can use to make changes, they can finally begin to put the right foot forward.

They often become great leaders once they finally settle down and embody their natural gift to create change for themselves and those around them.

The biggest thing for these individuals to focus on is to not just talking about endeavors that they might take on, but to actually take action in those endeavors. There must be a clear understanding that everything has happened for a reason.

It is also important for them to realize that they are also able to embody all of these experiences as tests along their journeys, and that they are able to harness the ability to achieve just about anything that put their minds to.

10/1 – Creative Inner Gift with Confidence

Having the opportunity to embody these energies is both a gift and a curse. Possessing a 0 means that there is something inherently special about you. What can be frustrating is that it takes a very long time to discover and develop this gift that you have been given.

As the 0 is surrounded by 1, this gift will definitely reflect creativity, but 1 will also bring a number of issues and tests that will constantly challenge these individuals.

When 1s can't find productive ways to release their creativity, they may lose confidence and find themselves over-indulging in addictive behavior. Many times they lash out when they are challenged because they lose a tremendous amount of confidence in themselves when they feel inferior.

When these individuals can establish a direction for productive ways to release their creativity, this gift that they are having trouble locating will present itself. Harnessing these energies in a positive and productive way will bring these individuals a sense of security and joy within their lives.

11/2 – Double Creativity with Confident Balance

To be ruled by this combination of numbers poses a huge challenge. With two 1s side-by-side, there is an emphasized desire to engage in addictive behaviors. This leaves these individuals with an extremely high sex drive.

Combining this with the number 2 presents the ability to get others to cooperate with their desires. These individuals can get into a lot of trouble if they are unaware of these powerful energies that they possess.

Competitive by nature, they will naturally find themselves resisting anybody that challenges them, especially when these outsiders are attempting to help them find structure within their lives. When these individuals are able to find productive ways to release their creativity daily, while also harnessing a sense of organization, they are able to create a thriving and confident reality.

Being productive and having variety in their lives is key for these individuals to create a healthy and balanced lifestyle for themselves.

12/3 - Creative Organization with Balanced Expression

Life is presented to these individuals through the fairy tale or tragedy scenario thanks to the number 3. What is beautiful here is the number 2's balance in conjunction with the confidence that the number 1 brings to the table.

These energies present themselves as a test. When life is perceived as a tragedy, these individuals have the tendency to complain. They also commonly lack confidence in themselves in situations in which they end up taking advantage of other people's kindness, while harboring a lot of resentment.

Being overly-sensitive to the way others feel has the potential to affect these individuals in either a positive or negative way depending on the people around them. In order for them to reach this fairy tale that they envision, they must surround themselves with people that influence them positively, and this will help them naturally feel better about their lives.

Creating a more organized lifestyle will help them be more productive as they release both their expression and creativity. In the end, this life is what you wish to make it. Therefore, engaging in a positive attitude will naturally bring peace to their minds.

13/4 – Creative Sensitivity with Expressive Process

The ability to feel and create a sense of stability for themselves within the structure of our society has the potential to manifest in many different ways both positively and negatively.

When life is not going as planned for these individuals, they tend to lack patience, which manifests as complaining and addictive behaviors. They often find themselves creating a great amount of doubt about how others view them and where they are headed in life.

Focusing on the abilities that they do have rather than what they don't have the ability to do will be very beneficial for this group of people.

This energetic combination requires the individual who is channeling it to be focused on a process in which the individual can release both their expression and creativity in positive outlets on a daily basis. When they are able to set a strong foundation for themselves that brings them both productive outlets in addition to a structured process of growth, these individuals will find the peace of mind that they have always been searching for.

14/5 – Creative Process with Stable Freedom

The creative process is a natural gift for these individuals, and the challenge for them is to balance their freedom with their discipline.

When they feel too free, carriers of a 14/5 usually lack structure and engage in addictive behaviors. Many times they depend on other people too much, and this leads them to be heavily judged by others while contributing to their lack of self-confidence.

When they find themselves to be too disciplined, they probably did go through a process and created foundations for themselves. They may, however, find that they tend to help others too much, and they can get trapped within this habitual tendency.

It is important for these individuals to focus on balancing their energies. When they are able to find this balance, they will see that their lives will manifest strong, productive images amongst their peers that allows them to feel confident and free at the same time.

15/6 – Creative Freedom with Disciplined Acceptance

These individuals are constantly challenged with how they find value within their daily creation.

Battling with their balance of freedom and discipline, these individuals, when over-free, can be extremely self-destructive and dependent on anybody they can find who is willing to help them. This can lead them to feel unmotivated, and it can lead them to addictive behaviors, and they usually gain confidence from this unhealthy behavior.

They live in the idea that if they never actually try, they can never truly fail. When this group of people can begin to find a sense of discipline in their lives, they can begin to visualize the right direction for themselves.

Using their strong minds and abilities to place value on their own lives, they can maintain a sense of balance when it comes to how much freedom they exert. This will instill a productive value system that will take them to great lengths within the structure of our society.

16/7 – Creative Vision with Intuitive Trust

This combination of numbers as a governing force can be both a gift and a curse. When manifesting positively, these individuals can envision a place of self-value for themselves in their lives that they know they are able to reach organically, rather than creating expectations for themselves.

On the other hand, when this negativity is persistent, they find themselves in situations in which they experience abandonment. This leads them to engage in destructive and addictive behaviors.

They tend to get lost in their own expectations of life and they continue to be too confident, and this causes others to see them as stubborn know-it-alls.

It is important to understand that abandonment is something that 7s naturally attract, and these individuals will be able to feel some peace of mind when it actually occurs.

Ultimately, looking for the positive side in every situation will help them accept their reality, and they will be able to discover the best ways to succeed when these circumstances arise.

17/8 – Confident Trust with Intuitive Abundance

This governing force presents the individual with an abundant energy that is driven through the creativity of their words and an inherited intuition that will manifest as heightened recognition. This recognition is both positive and negative, which is dictated by the individual's ability to process what they intuitively know they can create.

When they are able to exercise patience by being aware of all the necessary steps to achieve their goals, they will find more trust and confidence inside of themselves.

When they lack patience, however, they will find themselves engaging in more addictive behaviors, have issues with their personal power and how well they balance that with others, and find that they are creating abandonment in many aspects of their lives.

When this governing force trusts their intuitions and creates a process for themselves to take day-by-day, they find that they have more control over their realities, which will result in nothing less than an abundance of positive outlets for success.

18/9 – Creative Recognition with Inherent Wisdom

A well-recognized and amplified energy, these individuals will go through many challenging changes throughout the course of their lives. Stubborn and impatient, these individuals may find themselves engaging in addictive behaviors when they feel they have gotten too far ahead of the process and are not yet ready to take on leadership roles.

They may also carry a strong sense of arrogance because they can naturally feel that they are experiencing a much more amplified energy than most.

The 1 and the 8 together provide these individuals with the ability to attract a tremendous amount of recognition from others, whether they're looking for it or avoiding it.

The 9 influences change, and these individuals can react to their experiences in two possible ways. They can continue to stub their toes, being both overly-stubborn and arrogant, or they can gain lessons from their previous mistakes and become wise old souls that expand their integrity through their actions rather than just through their words.

It is important for these individuals to recognize that this is inevitable, and that this can help them create patience throughout their growth.

This will result in manifesting a higher understanding of the present moment and how they can achieve great success.

19/10/1 - Confident Wisdom with Creative Inner Gift and Confidence

An interesting challenge that these individuals are faced with is how and where they should release their creativity on a daily basis, while carrying the strong and stubborn energy of a 9. Creating a life that is immersed in good integrity keeps these people confident on the path to growth.

What tends to happen is that their world lacks the integrity that it once wished to have, which creates and addictive behavior that results in manipulation, arrogance and amplified change. It is imperative for them to realize that there are always going to be situations in which they are challenged by amplified experiences and change. This presents them with an opportunity to learn from their mistakes, while overcoming the hurdles that life throws at them.

They must remember that they have an inherited gift that, when discovered, will lead them to a more productive lifestyle that will be guided by the wisdom that they have gained throughout their process of growth.

20/2 - Cooperative Inner Gift with Balance

This combination of numbers is a unique gift that is strengthened by the ability to organize and gain cooperation from those around them.

What tends to be a huge challenge for these individuals is their ability to balance their giving and receiving.

When they give too much they feel resentment when it is not returned to them, and when they take excessively and do not return, others feel resentment toward them. This is usually the case when they are too organized and not open to allowing a moment to happen organically. It can also result from a lack of organization, and when this occurs these individuals tend to rely on others too much.

These individuals must be able to focus and understand that they have natural gifts, and when they reveal these gifts it will guide them to a much more productive and balanced lifestyle. When this occurs they will be able to achieve whatever they set their minds to.

21/3 - Balanced Creativity with Sensitive Expression

This experience is driven through productively organizing creative outlets of expression. These individuals can often find themselves in places where they complain about how life around them is making them off-balanced.

This is the reason they tend to find themselves engaging in addictive behaviors. They also can experience over-sensitivity to other people's energies, and this leads them to finding themselves at mercy to their demands.

It is important for them to recognize that they are instinctually in search of a fairy tale experience, and when this is not automatically presented to them, they turn to tragedy. This is what normally drives them into unproductive and manipulative behaviors.

When these individuals are able to understand that life is what they make of it, they are able to begin to discover that when they harness their inner creativity and ability to express themselves, they will certainly reveal this fairy tale that has always been right in front of them.

22/4 – Double Cooperative Balance with Stabilizing Process

This energetic combination thrives when it is complemented by a strong sense of identity that is created through patience and a well-balanced lifestyle.

Struggling with a balance of giving and receiving usually puts these individuals in situations of resentment and judgment. These situations will manifest in a way that is overly-dramatic, and that creates habits that do not coincide with a process and that lead the individual to rarely finish any project that they start.

When these individuals can realize that building a strong identity in our society begins with a well-organized and structured process, they will soon find themselves on a positive path. Knowing that there will always be hurdles that will challenge their stability will allow them to overcome this imbalance in order to create a positive process of execution no matter what the task may be.

23/5 – Balanced Expression with Disciplined Freedom

Finding a balance between how free and disciplined they will be on a daily basis is an important challenge for 23/5s.

When these individuals feel too much of freedom, they often lack independence and they tend to have other people cooperating with them. They also tend to use their natural sensitivity in order for other individuals to benefit emotionally.

On the other hand, when they are too disciplined, they find that their tendency to help others creates an avenue of dependence while also allowing others to take advantage of their sensitivity.

These are two extremes that, if balanced, will give them the power to create their own avenues of expression and freedom. In the end, when a healthy lifestyle is established, these individuals will understand their true value as human beings, and this will result in other people recognizing their value.

24/6 – Cooperative Process with Stable Acceptance

This combination of numbers is about creating a sense of value through visualizing a well-established and organized process.

Expectations tend to be the downfall here because these individuals are not happy with the particular way in which the process has unfolded. This creates a desire to criticize and judge those around them rather than accepting responsibility for how they have contributed to their lives and what they may perceive as misfortune.

This also forces them into very self-destructive behaviors that causes them to create resentment while lacking personal worth.

They have to realize that in order for them to live in a healthy and productive reality, they first and foremost need to accept things for the way that they are.

When they have done this they can begin the process of reorganizing their lives through a process that is well-executed step-by-step. Once these individuals get to this place they begin to find strength in both the process that they have chosen to build and the self-worth they gain from it.

25/7 – Balanced Discipline with Trusted Openness

Having the pleasure to experience this Ruling Energy leaves the opportunist with a strong sense of intuition, but the challenge is balancing their freedom with their discipline.

When these individuals lack discipline, they tend to get others to over-cooperate with them, therefore, this builds resentment that normally leads to abandonment. They may find themselves continuously searching for reassurance, as they feel that their peers are not always fully accepting of their actions.

Establishing a sense of balance in their lives will help them find a good and healthy amount of freedom. This freedom will be reflective of their discipline to be more organized.

When this is reached, they will be able to use the gift of intuition to create a reality for themselves that others can look to in order to receive help and guidance on the path to a higher understanding of life.

26/8 – Cooperative Vision with Abundant Recognition

This energetic experience presents individuals with the challenges of finding recognition throughout their daily lives, while also establishing a strong sense of self-worth.

Patience is a big factor with this energy, mainly because it takes time to visualize and execute a well-established plan to reach their fullest potential. What tends to occur here is an unrealistic expectation of how things should go, and when this expectation is not met, these individuals turn to self-destructive behavior.

This group of people tends to gain recognition in all the wrong ways. They must realize that they will naturally manifest an abundance of energy toward themselves when they are able to establish a good sense of balance with how they approach life. This leads to less resentment and fewer self-destructive behaviors while creating a level of acceptance for where they currently stand in life and how to grow in a productive way.

In the end, these individuals need to focus on balance with their giving and receiving. With this, they will realize that they are exactly where they need to be in their lives and the only direction they will be heading is up.

27/9 - Balanced Openness with Trusted Wisdom

These individuals are constantly tested with amplified experiences in order to gain wisdom, which normally reflects as some sort of abandonment.

This can be a very challenging reality when a 7 inherently knows that there's much more to this world than what they are led onto believe. The 9 either expands these individuals to search further or holds them back because of preexisting conditionings that reflect their integrity.

They often have issues with organization and imbalanced habits when it comes to giving and receiving, which leads to resentment.

When these individuals can trust their intuition and begin to see that what they are experiencing is there to teach them lessons of change and growth, they will step away from stubborn and hypocritical tendencies. This will manifest a more balanced and trusted lifestyle that others will look to for guidance.

28/10/1 - Cooperative Recognition with Creative Inner Gift and Confidence

With a very high instinct to compete for the amount of recognition they receive, these individuals can come off as pushy and power-hungry. On the other hand, when they lack confidence in themselves, they may find that they give their power away to others and refrain from getting involved in any type of competition due to the feeling that they already lost.

They may at times get stuck in addictive behaviors and find themselves building resentment both to and from others. The challenge here is to discover their inherited inner gifts in the realms of creativity, and then recognizing the steps needed to build those skills to their fullest potential. When this is established, these individuals find confidence and variety in their lives that creates a higher sense of abundance.

Point of Creation

2 – Cooperation and Balance

Possessing 2 as the Point of Creation only occurs when there is a combination of an Emotional Core of either 10/1, 19/101, 28/10/1, 37/10/1, or 46/10/1) paired with a Ruling Energy of 10/1, 19/10/1, or 28/10/1). So it's a fairly uncommon creation point to work from.

This creates a unique experience because 2's strength in organization is fueled by a vortex of immense creativity.

The biggest challenge for these individuals is being able to control the amount that they give and receive in any situation with which they engage.

With this Point of Creation, it is important to find balance within their lives, allowing them to have a sense of structure on a regular basis.

They must be aware that they will feel resentment at certain times, and that this is natural. Whether the resentment is coming from others or from themselves, it is important to be in control of these feelings, while thinking before they act.

This does not mean they should avoid feeling resentment. It is okay to feel this emotion, but they shouldn't stay stuck in it. This means allowing themselves to feel the emotion and, from there, ask themselves questions about where it is coming from in order to navigate it in a productive way.

If the resentment is not navigated in a productive way, this energy can get them into trouble.

When these individuals are able to discover a sense of balance while believing in themselves, they have immense power to manifest the most creative and fruitful reality. They must use this understanding to be more organized with their natural cooperative energy by living a more positive and productive lifestyle.

3 – Expression and Sensitivity

Working with a Point of Creation that channels expression and sensitivity is quite a task. These individuals tend to look at life in polarization, as if it were either a fairy tale or a tragedy. This leads them to want to access extreme highs and lows, using those opportunities as the building blocks for their life stories.

The most important challenge that this energy needs to overcome is the creation of doubt, which usually manifests as complaining and resisting change. The doubt also causes immense fear of change. A majority of this is driven from their sensitivity to any energy that is uncertain, that has the potential to lead them to misuse others.

In addition, they might also be misused by those around them. Discovering strength from inside of their own energy rather than relying on others for security will bring them strength while assisting in manifesting a much more calm, centered and controlled reality.

It is important for them to find productive outlets for expression because when that energy is blocked it many times results in a huge amounts of frustration. Many 3s deal with this issue because they get so immersed in each other's emotional states that they don't spend enough time focusing on themselves and what they need to release.

It is especially important when you have a Point of Creation of 3 that you give yourself time everyday to engage in your preferred outlets of expression. When you are able to find a rhythm within your life, your ability to create and express freely will come to you with ease and grace.

With the number 3 it is really all about being able to navigate your emotions productively, while allowing others to navigate their challenges on their own.

4 – Stability and Process

Having a Point of Creation that channels stability and a process is as simple as it sounds. The optimal reality for these individuals is one in which they will create a stable foundation and enjoy the process.

The most prevalent issue with 4s is that they struggle with patience, especially with the necessary steps needed to execute the process.

Since patience is key for carriers of 4s, they must first establish a vision for themselves. As long as it possesses direction, goals, and a process to follow, the type of lives that they create for themselves will find a natural rhythm for this group of people.

If only it was that easy for 4s to discover what their life purposes are, their lives would be a whole lot simpler. What happens with 4s is that they don't know the direction that they want to go and they tend to be very hesitant to actually take any leap one way or another. Because of this, they usually find small jobs that will keep them afloat while they continue to seek direction.

These individuals commonly create a lot of judgment toward other people and toward themselves. It is a common theme throughout the foundational numbers to identify with others based on the way in which society perceives them. This works both ways because whether it is positive or negative, 4s usually find themselves creating many types of labels and categories.

When 4s are able to be direct and become the people that they envisioned for themselves, life becomes very enjoyable for them. They become strong family figures, and they always lead by example.

Being true to themselves will instill a sense of pride for 4s. If they happen to stray from this path on which they are thriving, they have the potential to tear themselves apart.

Developing a positive state of mind in order to influence themselves and those around them positively will help 4s use their naturally judgmental energy productively.

5 – Freedom and Discipline

Having a Point of Creation of 5 is beautiful, but challenging. The challenge lies in a balance between freedom and discipline. Being too disciplined can result in a lot of frustration that is looking to be relieved by freedom. This search for freedom can be so intense that they many times search for it in other people, and when there is too much freedom they have the potential to become reliant on others, which can become unhealthy.

When there is a healthy balance within a 5, he or she can be one of the most dynamic creators that our planet has to offer.

Fives have a natural ability to entertain others, as they understand what fun is and how to create this setting for themselves and others. They have the power to create enormous amounts of joy, while discovering productive outlets in which they can let their energy of freedom run wild.

When it comes to discipline and 5s overcome their boredom, they have the potential to succeed in any activity into which they put their energy.

It is most difficult for them to stay committed to one activity, because 5s like to jump around from project to project. Some of the strongest and most talented people in our society have 5 as their Points of Creation.

These individuals find themselves with immense power to influence others, which gives them the opportunity to create a trajectory for themselves that will grant them the freedom that they have always desired.

6 – Vision and Acceptance

Channeling vision and acceptance through this Point of Creation is difficult because of self-worth, an energy that is very predominant in this energy.

Since 6 is about finding value from within, many times PoC 6s struggle to discover their self-worth. When they are uncertain about their value, they tend be very critical of others and focus on what others are not doing rather than taking accountability for what they are doing or not doing.

Sixes can also be very self-destructive, believing that if they never make a real commitment or effort, they will never have to face failure.

When 6s become comfortable with who they are, they become exemplary people within our society from whom we can learn, who support others in their processes while they carry out their own life journeys.

Six aligns with vision and acceptance because when these individuals are able to visualize and accept the people that they are, they can use this strength to help others in their development by being supportive of change and being comfortable with themselves.

Finding value in every situation by not setting expectations and allowing life to flow organically is a sign that a PoC 6 is on the right track.

7 – Trust and Openness

Those who create through trust and openness are challenged by 7s most prevalent issue: abandonment.

When you possess a 7 at any level, abandonment will occur in your life one way or another. When you create through this energy, abandonment will be a common theme throughout your life as long as your PoC is a 7.

Learning how to trust the universe is the first step in understanding what the energy of abandonment is trying to teach you. When you can let go of attachments to belongings or other people, you will soon find out that as one energy leaves, it brings the opportunity for new energies to enter.

7s have an extremely strong sense of intuition. This can often get them into trouble because they open up too much and tend to talk excessively. When 7s trust their intuition and learn how to use it properly, they will naturally attract the sort of individuals who not only want to hear what they have to say, but appreciate a sense of value from 7's inherent knowledge.

Seven is the most empathic number and, because of this, they always struggle with their feelings because they over-analyze situations too much. When this occurs, it is important for them to realize what they are doing while finding a productive way to navigate these thoughts.

All 7s need purpose in their lives in order to feel fulfillment. However, if PoC 7s don't have purpose, depression is almost a guarantee. Passion is what 7s must follow, because without it they will never feel that they have found a true purpose here on Earth.

Trust in the process of change and the development of a career is what all 7s must create for themselves to live prosperous, healthy, purpose-filled lives.

8 – Abundance and Recognition

Creating through abundance and recognition is about finding patience and understanding that carriers of an 8 will naturally create recognition for themselves. However, it's up to them as to whether it is positive or negative recognition.

PoC 8s struggle when they get ahead of themselves and feel that things should be handed to them. Since 8 is about the give and take of one power, those who create through 8 must find ways to take ownership of their inherent power and not give that strength to others.

Insecure 8s tend to only feel recognition through association. Because of this, they give their power away to others.

When 8s create their own sense of security, the power is their own and they are able to choose what to do with their energy rather than being told what to do.

PoC 8s especially need to understand that they are always going to be under some type of scrutiny whether they deserve it or not. This is part of having an abundant energy.

For 8, the key is understanding that natural abundance wants to find this group of people. The more they work toward creating a strong social identity for themselves, the more positive natural recognition will come their way.

PoC 8s can be some of the best examples of how to exercise patience while developing a strong identity for themselves within our society. It is important for them to believe that they can become pillars of success.

9 – Wisdom and Integrity

Creating through wisdom and integrity carries a tremendous amount of responsibility. Because the 9 is a mirror to others energies, when PoC 9s are off, they tend to cause others to follow suit. Nines will always have a strong influence on others, but when it occurs at the PoC level, there is a sense of responsibility that comes with it because they have the ability to grab onto others' energies immediately.

9 is about integrity, as it challenges its carriers to do the right thing and set the appropriate example.

Trouble will always find the number 9. This is okay as long as the 9 learns from mistakes and doesn't repeat the same mistakes over and over again. This is a common theme for 9, especially for those who create through this number.

PoC 9s may find themselves being very hypocritical because they use their ability to convince others while not actually practicing what they preach.

When 9s can discover who they are and learn how to live through high integrity, they will find themselves in positions of leadership and great responsibility. This is the type of energy in which these individuals will thrive if and when they learn from the mistakes that they have made and show their peers that they have made the necessary changes.

Amplified experience will naturally occur and, because of this, they must not allow those experiences to tear them apart. Instead, they should harness this energy and use it to gain wisdom to help the next soul who needs guidance through a similar experience.

PoC 9s have it all under control. They don't have to misuse it, otherwise, life will constantly be a struggle of change and criticism in relation to how they chose to spend their time here on Earth.

10/1 – Creative Inner Gift with Confidence

Those who create through the energy of 10/1 are blessed with incredible inner gifts in both creativity and confidence. When these individuals can develop confidence in the people they are by developing their inherent gifts, they are on the road to success.

An issue for PoC 10/1s is the actual discovery of those inherent gifts. This causes the major issues of the number 1 to rise, which are addictive behaviors, distracted realities, and manipulative creations.

When these individuals are insecure with themselves, they either are very clear with these issues or they do an incredible job of hiding them, due to their strength in manipulation. PoC 10/1s must focus on discovering who they are and why they are here because without that, realization of life will always be filled with conflict and deceitfulness.

When PoC 10/1s do discover who they are and what their gifts are, they are some of the most talented humans to walk the planet. They carry a sense of confidence that is not pushed upon others but is instead acknowledged.

Their creativity is alive and 10/1s naturally understand how to productively stimulate themselves with creative outlets rather than misuse this energy that normally leads to highly addictive activities.

If you are a PoC 10/1, you've got the juice. The challenge here is to discover that juice and use it as productively as possible. Focus, focus,

focus, and you'll achieve nothing short of greatness in whatever you put that focus toward.

11/2 – Double Creativity with Confident Balance

Having a Point of Creation energy of 11/2 is all about using creativity in a productive way while also developing organization throughout their everyday lives.

Having 1, a natural frequency, and 2, creative organization, takes a huge amount of organization. If this double frequency is not properly organized, this individual will experience great chaos and struggle.

It is important for them to find balance while engaging with whatever stimulates them. If they over-stimulate, however, the result can be just as negative as under-stimulating.

Creative structure will allow the number 2 to feel balanced and, therefore, provide productive outlets where they can be creative. When 11/2s create with confidence they're able to be productive contributors to any community.

When they are able to harness a strong sense of organization in conjunction with their natural creativity, they are very good at accomplishing any goals, whether they are individual or collective.

It is important for 11/2s to have healthy sex lives, and this is because 1s carry an amplified sex drive. If they are not able to find balance, then this will reflect in all aspects of their lives.

When these individuals are not confident they tend to use 1's manipulative ways to get others to over-cooperate with them, which leads them to resentment within their relationships.

Self-confidence is about believing in who they are, and when that belief is strong, they will not feel anxiety about other people and their intentions.

12/3 – Creative Organization with Balanced Expression

Having a Point of Creation of 12/3 is all about finding balance within self-expression.

People with the energy of the number 3 must remember that it is all about being aware of how sensitive they are to the energies that are around them and inside of them. When they are unable to balance what they feel, they will go through periods in which they lack self-confidence and will feel a great amount of frustration when attempting to express themselves.

12/3s must establish a belief in who they are, and from there they will be able to create confidence in how they express their feelings to the world.

When in the realms of doubt, this number can go through periods of high anxiety. Because the number 3 is hypersensitive to other people and their feelings, when they don't have a balanced understanding of what they're feeling they many times take on the stress of other people.

Since 3 has the ability to influence others by connecting with their emotions, 12/3s have a strong ability to manipulate others into cooperating with them. When these individuals develop a sense of confidence, they are able to use their abilities to influence others in positive and productive ways.

In order to create this confidence, these individuals must find comfort in their ability to express, which allows them to use their amplified sensitivity to help and contribute to others rather than complaining in order to manipulate others.

13/4 - Creative Sensitivity with Expressive Process

Those that have a Point of Creation of 13/4 are here to establish stability within their lives, which allows them to be confident in their expression.

Because the number 4 is very dramatic, this group of people tends to find themselves complaining and doubting the process that they are in. It is important for them to harbor patience, which allows them to develop confidence while standing on a stable foundation from which they can express themselves.

Choosing a process will give these individuals the confidence to take their journeys one step at a time. More often than not, 13/4s tend to take shortcuts because 4 can influence them to have a lack of patience, 1 creates a desire for more stimulation, and 3 creates doubt.

When these individuals are not able to find stability they tend to be very over-dramatic, which leads them to complain excessively while being displeased with life. This has the potential to lead to addictive behaviors that are actually subconscious cries for help.

While this group of people is in this doubtful vibration, they tend to judge others and blame those around them for their own dysfunction.

If they are able to develop a strong sense of confidence, they will gladly express themselves freely. Expression leads them to be confident in their journeys, and this process always leads to success for them. Ultimately, once they are able to properly express themselves they are able to harness the recipe for success, leading to much happier lives.

14/5 - Creative Process with Stable Freedom

Having a Point of Creation of 14/5 is quite interesting. The number 4 that is present here amplifies the desire to organize and process the world around them, while the 5 inspires the desire to be spontaneous.

Because of this, it is important for 14/5s to have confidence that the process of life will lead to great freedom – freedom that has longevity, rather than something that provides a quick fix.

The number 5 is known to get bored very quickly and, because of this, it can be difficult for this group of people to have faith in their journeys.

Often this these individuals will find themselves successful in many arenas, and because of this it is important for them to remain disciplined in order to flourish.

When these individuals establish a sense of discipline in their lives, they tend to be too free and have a thrill for drama. By utilizing 1's ability to influence others, they instinctively know how to trigger drama.

When they are unable to find stability, they tend to sway from highs and lows in self-esteem. This causes them to be confrontational because they might feel threatened by others that have a more stable energy.

Finding awareness of these tendencies allows them to find grounding in who they are, and they are able to start the process of being more disciplined, which will eventually lead to immense productivity and success.

15/6 – Creative Freedom with Disciplined Acceptance

Creating through the energy of 15/6 is about being consistent with discipline, which will bring these individuals to high levels of self-worth.

The number 6 struggles with failure, and as a result, a PoC 15/6 would rather just give up and be "free" than put in the work and potentially fail.

When PoC 15/6s accept what is in front of them as being exactly what they need, they establish confidence in themselves and find it much easier to be disciplined in what they are doing.

15/6s can face roadblocks in their creative journeys by being too critical of themselves, and this leads them to act too carelessly, seeking new outlets for stimulation. They can send themselves into a downward spiral when they set expectations that are too high for themselves, while failing to establish a sense of discipline that will help them properly execute their vision.

Finding hard work, confidence and dedication will lead them to a higher sense of self-worth. With this high self-worth, 15/6s will find it much easier to accept what comes their way by making the proper adjustments in order to be successful.

16/7 – Creative Vision with Intuitive Trust

Creating through 16/7 manifests as a test in developing trust by accepting change. When PoC 16/7s develop trust in their intuitions, they're able to visualize a path to success without issues making adjustments along that path.

Due to their strong intuitions, 16/7s can find themselves lacking purpose while cultivating personal value. This occurs because 6 struggles with self-worth while 1 desires confidence and, because of this, the intuition of a 7 seeks out materialistic outlets rather than those of high purpose. It is important for 16/7s to first establish a purpose for who they are and what they want to accomplish before they choose a direction.

When 16/7s are not confident in themselves and have low self-esteem, they tend to find themselves in situations of abandonment. Due to 7's need for trust, 16/7s find themselves looking to be reassured that they are in fact worthy of other people's time.

This may lead them to being manipulated because they want to trust and they want to be valued. As a result, they become too open and share too much while getting upset with others for not wanting to spend more time with them.

These individuals need to develop confidence and trust in who they are to build their own self-worth. This will then help them value their time, not needing the validation from others.

17/8 – Confident Trust with Intuitive Abundance

Those creating through the energy of 17/8 need to confidently trust their intuitions, and this will lead them to their natural abundance.

The number 8 draws a lot of attention and energy to it, so it is important for PoC 17/8s to not be too open because they lack confidence in themselves.

17/8s struggle with the process of developing their personal recognition because they do not trust themselves. This lack of trust can lead them to latch onto others for confidence and recognition. When PoC 17/8s develop their own confidence, they find it much easier to trust the process of life in full abundance.

These individuals tend to struggle with patience, which gets them into situations of abandonment, leading to addictive behaviors. Because 8s have strong energy fields, it can be difficult for 17/8s to control themselves. This lack of self-control can lead them to feel as if they have no purpose, which can lead into situations of isolation. When they are in this state, they will give up their power to anyone that will spend time with them, or anything that will stimulate them.

17/8s need to find purpose in the process that they wish to take. Establishing this purpose will give them confidence to create the natural and abundant reality into which they were born.

18/9 – Creative Recognition with Inherent Wisdom

Those who create through the energy of 18/9 are given a large responsibility of reflecting every individual's energy with which they come in contact.

At all three levels of the vortex (the final digit in their Emotional Core, Ruling Energy, and Point of Creation numbers), they possess a 9. We know this because the only single-digit numbers that equal 18 are 9 + 9, which would have to be the final digits in the EC and RE to create a POC of 18/9.

The result of having a 9 at all three levels of the vortex is that they reflect everybody else's fields. Carriers of these numbers should imagine themselves as giant mirrors for the emotions, experiences, and creations of others.

The most predominate energy of the number 9 is responsibility and, because of this, PoC 18/9s are naturally going to be in situations in which they are recognized for their integrity or lack thereof. It is extremely important for them to take responsibility for themselves and understand that their integrity will always be challenged.

When 18/9s struggle, they lack integrity in our world and, therefore, they find themselves in amplified situations in which they are recognized as examples of what not to be.

Lacking confidence and patience is usually the first step for 18/9s to head down the wrong path. These individuals will find themselves in many hypocritical situations that they tend to repeat. Taking responsibility for their actions will lead them to being productive parts of the community and the leaders that they were born to be.

Balancing Connections

This arena of energy encompasses how we connect with each other. The dynamics of our relationships work with all three of these energies (the Emotional Core, the Ruling Energy and the Point of Creation) helping all parties involved understand the energies that they are experiencing when they are together.

These concepts work in relationships that are one-on-one, but they also work in group settings. Understanding these connections is what allows each individual involved to have a higher awareness of what is being felt, experienced, and created through the connection between everybody involved.

How to Calculate:

At each energetic level, add each individual's final digit to the others involved.

Example 1:
Person 1: EC - 34/7, RE – 9, PoC - 16/7
Person 2: EC - 26/8, RE – 7, PoC - 15/6

EC connection = 15/6 7 + 8 = **15**
1 + 5 = **6**

RE connection = 16/7 9 + 7 = **16**
1 + 6 = **7**

PoC connection = 13/4 7 + 6 = **13**
1 + 3 = **4**

Example 2:

Person 1: EC - 35/8, RE - 14/5, PoC - 13/4

Person 2: EC - 29/11/2, RE – 8, PoC - 10/1

Person 3: EC - 24/6, RE – 6, PoC - 12/3

EC connection = 16/7 8 + 2 + 6 = **16**
1 + 6 = **7**

RE connection = 19/10/1 5 + 8 + 6 = **19**
1 + 9 = **10**
1 + 0 = **1**

PoC connection = 8 4 + 1 + 3 = **8**

Relationships

We all have connections with each other through our Zodiacs, elements, chakras and the three arenas of energy associated with our numbers.

Within those three arenas, if the relationship aligns with Emotional Core, it describes what the two people feel by being with one another. If it is aligned with Ruling Energy, it describes what the shared experience will be like. If it aligns with Point of Creation, it describes what the two will collectively create.

Here are the connections for one-on-one relationships. The minimum number that can be created is 2, and the maximum number that can be created is 18/9.

2 – Cooperation and Balance

It is important to focus on the balance of give and take that is present in this relationship. Together you'll be able to create organization for groups and create structure within your own lives.

When it comes to romance, it is a beautiful connection that will instill balance in each other's lives, leaving both of you with shared comfort.

This is a great connection for a work environment because it reflects organization and promptness.

3 – Expression and Sensitivity

It is important to identify the creation of doubt that you instill inside of one another. Together you'll feel an extreme emotional connection, and you will really enjoy being together one-on-one because you'll give each other a sense of comfort.

Romantically, there will be a deep connection and an enhanced sensitivity for how one another feels. In saying that, be aware that your partner will be able to naturally sense how you feel in any moment. If misinterpreted, it can reflect as doubt that they will project onto you.

Business-related situations can be very difficult here due to the doubt that is shared, which in turn makes it very difficult to come to any sort of shared conclusions.

4 - Stability and Process
It is important to focus on being patient with one another.

You'll both find that you have a strong sense of identity when you are together. This is to the point that when you spend time together socially, people look at the both of you in a particular way.

Romantically, it's important not to get too far ahead of yourselves, because this will create conflict. It is important to remain in the present moment as much as possible.

This will be a very strong business relationship because these individuals have the ability to understand economics with ease while identifying areas in which they will prosper. Creating an economic foundation together is very possible if you can have the patience to take the necessary steps to reach your overall goals.

5 - Freedom and Discipline
It is important for individuals who are in a relationship of this dynamic to be careful of getting into trouble with one another. On the other hand, they have the potential to experience a lot of fun together. They can also share a disciplined lifestyle when they together.

Helping others together is a strength that is harbored in this relationship, as well as the desire to help each other.

On the romantic side, this relationship tends to fit the "fling" category, due to the freedom that is present. It also can be a great connection for two people that are looking to create a shared discipline in their lives.

This is a very productive working relationship when boundaries are created between the work environment and the social realm. If this is not created, it can reflect as conflict through the intent to discipline the other person.

6 - Vision and Acceptance

Finding a level of acceptance with each other's particular lifestyle is important in this dynamic. When this does not occur, this can create a great deal of criticism that is directed toward one another.

In addition, when they are together, it is very easy to sit back and criticize the world around them, which they always see as an entertaining time.

Romantically, they will both feel like the other person is the perfect match. As they spend more time together it is important to be aware that their original expectations toward one another will never actually be met. Finding a way to accept one another for who they are will create longevity here.

In the business realm, this is a great pairing to reveal flaws and values within the work environment. It is extremely important to create positive criticism in order to get the most out of each other.

7 - Trust and Openness

With an intuitive connection, together you are able to anticipate what is to come in the future. With that said, it is important not to get too far ahead of yourselves because abandonment tends to occur quite often in your lives.

Not creating attachments to one another and being aware that you can always reconnect later in your lives is the key to having peace of mind in this relationship.

Romantically, an instantaneous connection is created that both of you can intuitively feel. The fear of separation is naturally instilled within both of you and is the root of any conflict that may arise.

Business-wise, the relationship is only successful when both people have a strong sense of trust in each other, so be open and honest and find creative ways to work through any issues.

8 – Abundance and Recognition

Both individuals have a sense of social recognition as a result of the presence of the other person.

The biggest test within this setting is the balance of power and control between each other.

Focusing on the fact that abundance is inevitable will bring a sense of peace to both parties.

Romantically, the level of social recognition is extremely high and, because of this, at times you may be into each other for other external reasons as opposed to being motivated by a pure emotional connection.

This will be an incredible business relationship since natural abundance is manifesting in your lives, and together you'll have an in-depth sense of social value and how to channel this to your advantage.

9 – Wisdom and Integrity

This relationship renders amplified experiences and, as a friendship, this partnership will lead to a lot of lessons learned with one another. You'll often find yourselves challenging the other's particular ways of life, often reflecting as stubbornness from both sides.

It is important to focus on growth through lessons and understanding that will come from your shared experiences.

Romantically, a strong, immediate connection will occur. This has the potential to quickly reflect as doubtfulness of the purity of the connection as well as criticism of one another that stems from this doubt. If this barrier is conquered, an incredibly strong connection is created that can withstand whatever comes your way.

On the business side, it is a very effective relationship when it comes to strengthening your economic value. However, if integrity is not practiced, it can destroy the business and the relationship.

10/1 - Creative Inner Gift with Confidence

There will be an inner spiritual connection in this relationship, and they'll both feel that they may have met each other before.

Together, these two individuals will be very creative in whatever they get involved with. Being aware that they instill confidence within one another is important, because when they lack confidence in one another conflict will arise.

Romantically, this is an extremely deep soul connection due to the inner gift that is present. The creativity will amplify each of their sex drives, and it will be very important to be physical with each other on a consistent basis.

Business-wise, they'll get along well and can be very creative together, but it is important to build confidence within their shared ideas. If this does not occur, it can create a disconnection and a loss of collective creative savvy.

11/2 - Double Creativity with Confident Balance

Amplified creativity and a lot of confidence is harbored within both of you. Issues will tend to arise and the lack of cooperation between you will begin to reveal itself.

Focusing on balancing your giving and receiving between one another will lead to a more consistent level of confidence within this relationship.

Romantically, this is an extremely amplified sexual connection, tending to reflect as instantaneous physical attraction and activity. For this to work, it is of the utmost importance that each of you makes the necessary sacrifices in order to balance out your sex life and the amount of quality time you spend together building a mental connection.

On the business side, this can be a very creative relationship when it comes to collaborating to build organization in any business-type setting.

12/3 - Creative Organization with Balanced Expression

This will manifest as a sensitive, very emotionally-connected relationship. Here, you'll find that you really enjoy one-on-one time together.

On the other side of that, you'll be challenged in the realm of giving and receiving between the two of you, which will directly reflect in the confidence that you two will share.

Romantically, this can be a great relationship to share a deep, sensitive connection together, while also sharing a more balanced and confident lifestyle.

On the business side of things, it can work only when there is an open, positive arena for expressive cooperation. If this does not occur, it tends to build resentment in both parties until a lack of confidence is created.

13/4 - Creative Sensitivity with Expressive Process

Creating an emotionally-connected state of stability is the essence of a successful relationship here. It is important to be aware that issues with confidence and doubt will spark this lack of stability between you. It's important to be patient with one another, which in turn will help remove doubt and build a stable foundation between you.

On the romantic side of things, instilling a stable foundation is extremely important when it comes to building a doubt-free, confident connection.

Business-wise, this is a great relationship since the two of you can naturally feel what is needed to succeed within our society's framework.

14/5 - Creative Process with Stable Freedom

Creating a stable, confident connection is essential for a healthy, freedom-based relationship.

When confidence is lost, an impatience with each other can arise with a desire to discipline the other person. Be aware that this pairing can also get in trouble if they're not careful.

Romantically, this relationship can be a lot of fun since they both enjoy social, freedom-based settings and will also instill a sense of social identity and confidence with one another.

Business-wise, it is important to create a sense of discipline within each other, which will directly build a confident, step-by-step process to achieve their collective goals.

15/6 - Creative Freedom with Disciplined Acceptance

Confidence with each other can create a number of productive, freedom-based settings through shared discipline.

Together, it is very easy for you to criticize the world around you and those involved in it. Be careful of being too critical of each other, as it will only reflect as a lack of confidence and will lead to conflict between you.

Romantically, this will instantaneously feel perfect, but as time evolves, you'll find that you are both trying to discipline each other to act the way you originally pictured each other. It is extremely important to accept one another for who you are for this to withstand any type of longevity.

On the business side of things, a great working environment is created when discipline is implemented, which in turn will create a nearly flawless result if and when confidence is instilled with each other.

16/7 - Creative Vision with Intuitive Trust

Creating confident acceptance of each other with a shared vision of how to coexist together will manifest a trusting reality.

Opening up to a shared confidence will create an intuitive sense of understanding between you. Be careful not to create abandonment, because it can reflect as a lack of confidence and a loss of trust with one another.

Romantically, this can be a very strong, intuitive connection that can result in being a perfect match. In saying this, it is even more important to make sure that abandonment is not going to take place. If it does occur, it is important to remember that you can always come back to each other down the road, and knowing this can be very helpful.

Business-wise, this is a great working relationship when trust is developed, creating a very positive, critical outlook on the task at hand.

17/8 - Confident Trust with Intuitive Abundance

Possessing a creative, intuitive trust together can lead to a deep connection between the two involved in this relationship.

Issues may arise when the idea of extended separation arises. This can lead to having to confront issues of power and control when it becomes time to discuss what each individual's next move will be.

It is important to remain aware that the illusion of abandonment exists and that, in the end, abundance is inevitable for this pair. Having this awareness can bring confidence to the parties involved.

Romantically, the connection is strong on both ends. In addition, a sense of social imagery can be created, as others tend to admire these partners as a power couple.

In this pairing, a very strong business relationship is created. Abundance is created by a confident foundation based on an intuitive outlook on the steps needed to reach the ultimate goal.

18/9 – Creative Recognition with Inherent Wisdom

Focusing on the balance of power and control over their experiences is extremely important when it comes to instilling confidence in one another. This allows the pair to be very creative with how they attract attention.

In addition, all of the experiences shared will be amplified in order for each of them to learn lessons and gain wisdom.

Romantically, they'll both feel a strong sense of social recognition, which will ultimately instill confidence in them both. The connection will be very strong for both parties when they break through the doubt and critical boundaries that usually exists in the beginning of the relationship.

On the business side of things, this is an extremely successful pairing when they understand that abundance is inevitable. A balance of power must also be instilled between them. Amplified, confident recognition will be achieved through a solid, patient, and well-structured process.

Growth Cycles

The Growth Cycles are the cycles that we are tested and challenged by every year.

They work in three levels. One level changes every year on the day that you were born, and the second shifts every 9 years. The third level works through the creation energy based off of where you are at in your current emotional and ruling cycle.

Each individual, depending on what Emotional Core he or she enters the planet with, starts his or her first full lifecycle from ages 0-8. Therefore, unless you enter the planet with an Emotional Core of 1, you're entering the planet in the middle of what we will identify as your "0" lifecycle.

The number of your Emotional Core determines the point in which you begin your first lifecycle. For example, if you've entered the planet with an Emotional Core of 4, this means that you're in the 4th year of your 0 lifecycle when you are born. Because the lifecycles come in periods of 9 years, you must complete years 5-9 before you would begin your 1st official lifecycle. Since you were completing the last portion of your "0" lifecycle from ages 1-5, you would begin your first lifecycle at the age of 6.

The third level, creation, works in the same way that it does for your personal energy; just as you have the EC, RE and PoC for you personally, those same aspects also apply to your growth cycles.

The lifecycles are also significant because they create a Point of Creation vortex. For example, if you were in your 3rd cycle and your 4th year, your PoC would be 7. This works for each cycle and each year.

It is so important to take notice of the PoC because as each year passes, we are faced with different tests in the three arenas of energy. The vortex of those arenas also gives us opportunities to experience a year of someone else's emotions. For example, in the vortex of 3, 4, and 7, that person will experience what it is like to be a 34/7. The growth through theses cycles is not just personal but also gives us an opportunity to understand our peers.

To receive information about the energy associated with Point of Creation, refer to the Point of Creation sections ranging from 2 through 18/9.

To learn about more about growth cycles in general and determine where you are in your life currently, visit our website at http://newearthconnect.com.

Emotional Growth Cycle Years

The emotional cycles of growth occur throughout your entire life in periods of 9 years. The overall goal is to reach your 9th full lifecycle, which starts from ages 72 to 80 depending on what your core numbers are.

Each lifecycle is an opportunity to prepare for year 8, the year of abundance, while also gaining wisdom from the past 8 years during the 9th year.

When this cycle is over, you will repeat the cycle again back at year 1, building a new trajectory through lessons learned over your next 9 years.

Each individual year will represent an area of focus in order to be successful within this time period.

1 - Creativity and Confidence

The focus of this year will be how to build self-confidence by finding ways to release creativity daily. Being aware that you'll have an amplified sex drive as well as being more susceptible to addiction can help you understand how to approach these urges constructively.

This is a great year to be creative and find new hobbies in addition to new ways to succeed within other realms of life. Make sure that you maintain variety in your daily life.

2 - Cooperation and Balance

The focus of this year will be to constructively find balance in your giving and receiving. Be wary of the fact that failing to find balance can create resentment toward others or from others, depending on which side you lean toward.

It is a great year for bringing people together and organizing your life through cooperation, whichever way you may use it to your advantage. It is important to refrain from over-cooperating.

3 - Expression and Sensitivity

The focus for this year is to find productive ways to express yourself, and be aware that over-sensitivity will be an issue. Remaining aware of this will allow you to realize that it is important for you not to block your expression and allow yourself to release your sensitivity.

It is a great year to reestablish one-on-one connections with old friends as well as make new connections.

It is important to refrain from creating doubt.

It is also significant to note that you have an amplified ability to pick up emotions from other people during this year.

4 – Stability and Process

The focus of this year is to begin laying down a foundation to create a more improved self-image.

You'll find that this year will be like a fountain of great ideas running through your mind about how to improve your life. Be aware that a step-by-step process is necessary for any great idea to become a reality, and it is important to create this success.

It is also important to refrain from having a lack of patience throughout your days.

5 – Freedom and Discipline

The focus of this year is to establish discipline within the foundation that you began the following year. Being able to accomplish this on a daily basis will further allow you to experience more freedom in the future.

It is a great year for creating fun experiences for yourself and others, as well as helping other people overcome their personal issues.

It is imperative to refrain from over-disciplining yourself while being wary of how your boredom creates an unhealthy amount of freedom.

6 – Vision and Acceptance

The focus of this year is to visualize how to perfect your self-image by accepting what you have created over the past five years. Be aware that criticism and self-worth are at the forefront of this year, and it is important to try to remain on the positive side of both.

This is a great year to make changes within your life by identifying your imperfections and then focusing on how to productively make the necessary changes. Refrain from setting expectations.

7 – Trust and Openness

The focus of this year is to trust your intuitions and further apply them to what you have been creating over the past six years.

Be aware that the downfall of this year will be the fear of abandonment, so it is important to focus on what is actually occurring throughout your daily life because that abandonment is always self-created.

This is a great year to really open up your expression through your ability to trust yourself. Stay away from needing reassurance and expressing more than is necessary.

8 – Abundance and Recognition

Finally you have made it to the year of abundance. The focus will be how you will receive recognition for what you have developed over the past seven years.

Since opportunities will be coming your way throughout this year, it is important to involve yourself in the most positive experiences. Recognition isn't always in the form of positive abundance.

This year is a great opportunity to really elevate your life and establish a firm foundation that can create longevity of wealth in many different forms. Refrain from overpowering others and attempting to control every situation that comes your way.

9 – Wisdom and Integrity

The focus of this year stems from your past eight years, which manifests itself in a number of amplified experiences that reflect drastic change in your life. It is extremely important to be aware that the reason for these changes is to gain further wisdom from each and every experience.

This is a great year to reflect on this past full lifecycle in order to learn as many lessons as possible.

Refrain from holding attachments to people or anything that is extremely important to you. Remember, everything happens for a reason, and value can be found in any situation, you just need to look for it.

Ruling Growth Cycles

Each cycle extends for the duration of 9 years and acts as the Ruling Energy that you will channel. These cycles start at different ages for everybody depending on the emotional number with which you enter the planet.

The age of emotional core when your first full growth cycle begins would be:

1- birth	4- 6	7- 3
2- 8	5- 5	8- 2
3- 7	6- 4	9- 1

At the end of the 4th cycle, you shift ruling and creation energies inside of yourself, which is the Point of Shift in your lifecycle. However, we'll go into that in more detail later.

Each ruling growth cycle has certain characteristics, as described in what follows.

0 – Inner Gifts

Besides those who are born into year 1 of their lifecycle, everybody will experience at least one year in their 0 lifecycle at the beginning of their lives. This cycle is never a full 9 years, which makes it unique among the various growth cycles, which is why it works with the energy of zero.

Zero expands inner gifts at a very young age. It also affects the maturity levels because it either gives people a head start within their growth cycles or a late start.

The numbers 2, 3 and 4 can especially show a lot of signs of immaturity early in their lives, but they also have tremendous amounts of talent that they become aware of at a very young age.

Two great examples of individuals who have experienced this are Kobe Bryant and Lil' Wayne, who are both 38/11/2. Because of this number combination, they didn't begin their first full growth cycle until they were 8 years old. Although it may have put them behind when it comes to maturity, it also granted them tremendous gifts on which to focus. Today they are both in their 4th full lifecycles, and they are considered the greatest in their crafts.

Wherever each individual begins his or her respective journey of growth here on this planet, it is important to be aware of this because it will help him or her understand the energetic challenges that each of us faces.

1 - Creativity and Confidence

The first cycle can fall between birth and 16 years of age.

This cycle is about establishing confidence from within and in relation to life around you. This occurs throughout childhood, when all of our natural creative tendencies are being established.

We all begin to develop our respective passions and face tremendous amounts of challenges with confidence throughout this time period. This is when we are challenged competitively, get introduced to sexuality, find different modes of stimulation, and go through hormonal changes in our minds and in our bodies. All of this is a reflection of the energy that we hold.

Raising children today with this awareness, you will be able to understand what energetic changes your child is going through while finding ways to continue to build his or her confidence.

2 – Cooperation and Balance

The second cycle can fall between 9 and 25 years of age.

In this cycle you begin to establish your habits in relation to cooperation. You develop direction through the confidence you have built throughout your first cycle.

In this period of time you also find balance in the way you want to live and the person you want to become.

The issue during this cycle is lack of cooperation, and this is caused when confidence is not cultivated in any particular direction during the first lifecycle. It's important to be aware that this cycle presents a lot of lessons in realms of choice as well as give and take with others.

Establishing a sense of independence and direction is the underlying goal for this cycle.

3 – Expression and Sensitivity

The third cycle can fall between the ages of 18 and 34.

This cycle is often the time period in which we are searching for love, the perfect mate with whom to start a family. You can see this reflected in the number 3's energy of influencing either fairy tale or tragedy.

Themes that occur throughout this cycle include tests of the heart, falling in and out of love, going through stages of intense sexual expression or being celibate and, lastly, attempting to establish a comfortable role within society.

Some of the biggest tests come through navigating a great deal of self-doubt in who you are. Because the previous two cycles are about establishing who you are, the third is about deciding whether or not you like who you have become.

Here you will either continue on the path you've been on your entire life or you'll dig deeper into yourself in order to become a new you.

4 - Stability and Process

The fourth cycle can fall in between the ages of 27 and 43.

It marks the end of the early stages in life. You are now ready to establish some sort of identity here and begin the process of building your own family.

This cycle is all about establishing a foundation in your life while becoming a productive member of society. It's also a cycle that will be filled with high levels of drama if you don't enter with a good head on your shoulders.

It's important to be patient with life during this cycle, as it will naturally progress for you based on how much you have grown throughout the previous three cycles.

As this cycle concludes, it marks the point at which your personal Ruling Energy shifts from the day and month of your birthday to the year in which you were born. This in turn will also shift your Point of Creation and will change your ruling and creation relationships with everybody.

5 – Freedom and Discipline
The fifth cycle can fall between the ages 36 and 52.

This cycle marks the beginning of a new you and a new energy that you possess. Because of this new energy, you may begin to question yourself and your relationships with others.

If something is off in your relationships, it will certainly surface during this cycle. This tends to be a breaking point in many marriages, as people tend to grow apart from each other during this time period because they want freedom back in their lives.

The most important thing to focus on is finding a strong balance between freedom and discipline within your life. If you find yourself trying to save a relationship, space and allowance can be the best healing methods for people to work out their own issues inside of themselves.

6 – Vision and Acceptance
The sixth cycle can fall between the ages of 45 and 61.

This is a time in life when your work usually pays off, and this is also the period in which you have left your mark on the world, no matter what this mark may be.

The energy of this cycle can also be very self-destructive and can lead to a time when you may fall under heavy scrutiny. It is important to take action in what makes you happy while establishing personal value. The outside world will either commend your accomplishments or expose your lack of accomplishment.

Divorce is a common theme during this time in people's lives, so be wary of this as it may happen to you and those around you.

7 - Trust and Openness

The 7th cycle can fall between the ages of 54 and 70.

This is normally a time when people retire from their professions in life. As seven is the most spiritual number, many people start to understand death during this time and begin their transitions into the later stages of life.

It's important to focus on the aspects of life that you enjoy and the individuals who are still a part of it.

Establishing trust that you are a soul first and a body second will allow your mind to not focus on physical death, but instead enjoy the time left here to the fullest.

8 - Abundance and Recognition

The eighth cycle can fall between the ages of 63 and 79.

This is a time in life when most are retired and are enjoying life to the fullest. Abundance is key here, and hopefully by this time in your life money is no longer an issue. Life should be abundant during this time, full of family and grandchildren.

It is essential to understand that recognition and care are important during this stage of life. People that reach this level need support from those around them but also offer great support to others on their journeys.

9 - Wisdom and Integrity

The ninth cycle falls between the ages of 72 and 88.

Congratulations if you have made it this far, as your energy has entered a time of great wisdom. All of this has developed from your integrity, which has grown over the previous 8 cycles.

This is often a challenging period with health, and it will bring a tremendous amount of change. It is important to get the most out of every day and find avenues to share all that you have gained throughout your life.

Your influence is now your strongest gift, so utilize it to help others find purpose and direction along their journeys.

Point of Shift (PoS)

As you have seen earlier, your Ruling Energy shifts halfway through your life. The point at which the Ruling Energy shifts is not the same for everybody, but is determined by what we will call the Point of Shift (PoS).

The PoS always occurs after the completion of the 4th full lifecycle. Therefore, having an understanding of lifecycles and how an individual's placement within his or her lifecycle is determined by his or her Emotional Core, you can now identify when your PoS would occur.

Knowing when your PoS occurs will help you utilize your Ruling Energy and your Point of Creation when it shifts part-way through your life. (Your Point of Creation also shifts when your Ruling Energy shifts because PoC is calculated by adding your RE with your EC.)

Here are the ages at which the shift occurs based on knowing the last digit of your primary Emotional Core number.

1- 36 yrs	4- 42 yrs	7- 39 yrs
2- 44 yrs	5- 41 yrs	8- 38 yrs
3- 43 yrs	6- 40 yrs	9- 37 yrs

No number ends in 0.

So, if your EC = 34/7, the Point of Shift is at 39 years old (based on the information above), and an EC of 38/11/2 is at 44 years old.

Worldwide Daily Energy

This energy affects the every single human being on the planet day in and day out. Holding all three energetic fields, we as a collective are moving through constant energetic change from day to day and year to year. Becoming aware of this energy helps us understand why certain events take place within certain days and also gives each individual an opportunity to seize the day and apply himself with his best foot forward.

How to Calculate:

Add up the desired date in the same form you would to decipher an individual being born on that particular day.

Example 1:

Date: 1/15/2015

EC connection = 15/6 1 + 1 + 5 + 2 + 0 + 1 + 5 = **15**
1 + 5 = **6**

RE connection = 7 1 + 1 + 5 = **7**

PoC connection = 13/4 6 + 7 = **13**
1 + 3 = **4**

To determine the ruling number for the current year, simply calculate it based on the digits of the year.

2015 is ruled by 8 2 + 0 + 1 + 5 = **8**

Example 2:

Date: 9/27/1985

EC connection = 41/5	9 + 2 + 7 + 1 + 9 + 8 + 5 = **41** 4 + 1 = **5**
RE connection = 18/9	9 + 2 + 7 = **18** 1 + 8 = **9**
PoC connection = 14/5	5 + 9 = **14** 1 + 4 = **5**
1985 was ruled by 23/5	1 + 9 + 8 + 5 = **23** 2 + 3 = **5**

Part IV.
The Application of Healing

Sacred Sexuality

Sex is an essential part of our beings for a multitude of reasons. Through the common perception, sex is the medium through which we receive pleasure, and it is also the means through which we perpetuate our species through reproduction. The real fact of the matter is that sex offers us more than just pleasure and reproduction.

By having sex that is high-energy, we can elevate our vibrations and the vibrations of our partners. Commonly, many of us are only interested in our partners because of their physical appearances. There is nothing wrong with being very attracted to your partner, and there is nothing wrong with seeking a very attractive partner, but the key to elevating both of your vibrations is being connected energetically.

Many people meet someone that they like and they immediately rush into sex because this is the only way that they know how to show affection. The act of sex is all about sharing energy with your partner, so if the two of you have not fully gotten to know and hone your personal energies, exchanging energy can have a negative effect.

It is vital to take time to understand how your personal energy works and then discover how your partner's energy works. By engaging in both breathing and meditative practices, both you and your partner can become much more comfortable with linking energies. Then, when you engage in sex, the energy that you pass between one another will be more beneficial to your personal energy fields.

With sex, you actually exchange confidence levels with your partner. Because of this, if one partner is more confident than the other, one partner is actually on a higher vibrational frequency. As a result, if you have sex and exchange your energies, the individual that is on a higher frequency will pass that to his or her partner and vice versa. In turn, the partner that had a higher level of confidence will be brought down to a lower frequency, and the other partner will gain an energy boost.

Discover your own level of self-confidence and from there find the person who matches your level and is eager to expand with you. Through sex, you can either raise your vibration or lower it, the choice is yours.

We all have male and female energies inside of us. Some men are more feminine than most and some women are more masculine than most, but it is important to understand which partner in the relationship is holding which energy.

Sometimes the two of you will jump back and forth, which is perfectly fine, but it is important to uplift your partner in order to step into the energy in which he or she feels most comfortable. As time goes on, the two of you will begin to gain a greater understanding of which energy each of you prefers.

We are now going to discuss a medium of sacred sexuality called Ankhing, which derives from ancient Egypt.

This is a process in which the orgasm releases from the sex chakra and returns back into the body. Instead of leaving the body, this allows the individuals who are engaged in the act to raise their vibrations.

As human beings, we release physical ejaculations when we orgasm and energetic ones that are lost when they leave us through our crown chakras. Ankhing allows us to retain the energy in our bodies, so as the orgasm reaches the heart chakra, we are able to push it out of our backs, up and around our heads, and then back into the heart chakra.

By doing this, we are not releasing our energy to our partners, but keeping it inside of our own energetic bodies. This helps us stay youthful and healthy, while also helping us stay on a higher vibration, keeping our energy levels higher as well.

In order to have total control over this energy, one must have a fully open and connected relationship with his or her partner, one that is focused on linking up with each other's breath during sex.

As we look again at the idea of love, we must understand that all of our physical relationships are opportunities for growth. Not until you fully develop love inside of yourself will you find the right partner with whom to commit and build a family.

People often jump into relationships for the wrong reasons. Whether the reason is financial, physical, fear of being alone, validation, or anything that does not have to do with the equal exchange of love and collective spiritual growth, it will negatively affect your personal energy and those around you.

If you're in a negative energetic relationship and you bring children into this world, they will be forced to grow up in a poor energetic environment, embodying the negative energies that they have learned from their parents.

Our main focus with this information about energy is to affect the children on this planet so they are no longer conditioned into negative, self-indulgent, separated energies.

The impact we wish to leave is one in which personal energies are understood at a young age, and productive, unified, personal habits are established at the beginning of people's lives.

The Application for Change

Applying this knowledge is not something that comes easily. At first, some of this information can be overwhelming because of our newfound ability to see insecurities that lie inside of ourselves or others.

The key to understanding the CTYS system is to focus on yourself while observing the life around you.

By being more positive and by focusing on personal growth and success, your energy will radiate to those around you, and they will then become more balanced.

When people first learn the CTYS system they tend to focus too much on other people's behavior while failing to work on themselves. It is important to understand that this is first and foremost a tool to improve ourselves, rather than pointing out the flaws in those around us.

Once you have been working with CTYS for some time and you have worked on yourself to a certain degree, then you can use it to help others.

It is important that we do not judge others once we have this information about them. We must use it to empathize with them and understand why they are the way that they are, and from there we can help them navigate whatever challenges they are facing.

In addition, by working on yourself first, you serve as an example for others, and they can learn from you by observing your actions.

It is also important to remember the Law of Attraction and that we create our own realities. When we understand energy, we have a huge advantage. When you apply this knowledge to yourself, you can positively create the reality that you want and this will inevitably lead to abundance and peace.

A large part of applying this information is first grasping what is actually transpiring throughout our society today. The reason we have chosen to expose how the conditioning process has developed is to show our readers that change is a necessity.

In order for us to ever be able to fully apply this knowledge as a collective, we must all be aware that the current infrastructure of our society is not created for the greater good of all. Instead, it flourishes through greed, power, and separation.

Unfortunately at this current time in our existence, immediate change can only be created through chaos.

History has shown us that chaos always results in drastic change, therefore, chaos is what those in current positions of power use to keep us in fear and under control.

The difference between 2015 and previous time periods is that we as human beings are in the midst of a process of evolution with a trajectory to create drastic positive change on this planet. In order for us to ever get to this change, we as individuals must find a way to decondition ourselves from any thoughts that separate us from each other.

We have always been rooted in protecting our own. It's one of our greatest instincts. We must realize that "our own" is all human life on this planet and, as a collective, we are not protecting our own right now.

We need to establish a better system of functioning as a society that does not leave anybody in situations in which they cannot comfortably exist.

Our system has always been reward-based, and the more you accomplish the more financial success you will receive. The more financial success you receive the better opportunities you will create for your family.

This was a great system when the Founding Fathers first established the United States and opportunity was an abundance. The Founding Fathers did not create our laws with the vision that we would have cars, phones, internet, and great advancements in human life.

It is foolish that we as a society are still following rules and regulations that were established 400 years ago.

Our world is now stronger than it has ever been, filled with many extremes. From lavish lifestyles to the starving poor, we as a collective do not have any true core value system.

A majority of our world is a made up of lies and agendas. Everybody presents themselves with some level of grey in order to mask who they truly are. This is never going to change until we all begin to collectively desire a better world.

How do we find resolution through a system that has been built for centuries through delusion and separation?

We must become aware of the true nature of our world and our connection to earth as a society. We must empower those who wish to create change. Rather than revolting, we play their game and we play it well.

Money is currently what controls energy on this planet more than anything else. For us as a society to create this change, we must participate and do well within the system of currency in order to give us the opportunities we need to create mass change.

Imagine a world that has no struggle. It has no need for crime because the need for desperation has been removed. Everybody has a purpose and function within a greater society; a society in which we are all educated about energy, in which we are all fully abundant, in which our basic human needs are taken care of, and in which we all have the opportunity to choose a path of purpose that contributes to the greater good.

We are the 99%, and we have the choice to create any world that we desire.

Those in control have created a world that revolves around themselves, and the rest of us must abide by their rules and regulations. It's not about revolting. It's about gradual, productive change to empower those with the highest integrity. We have to find a collective resolution that will allow the entire world to function as one productive love-driven society.

We have come so far as a society, and within that journey our souls have learned and experienced a tremendous amount of pain and suffering.

It is the beginning of the end of collective imbalance and extreme individual power. We will evolve into a society that is driven through love and integrity. We will find solutions that reflect love and unity as a collective. Most importantly, we will learn that we are all created through love.

Bibliography

Frissell, Bob. *Something in This Book Is True*. Berkeley, CA: North Atlantic Books, 2003.

Marciniak, Barbara, and Tera Thomas. *Bringers of the Dawn: Teachings from the Pleiadians*. Santa Fe, NM: Bear, 1992.

Millman, Dan. *The Life You Were Born to Live: A Guide to Finding Your Life Purpose*. Tiburon, CA: HJ Kramer, 1993.

Pouba, Katherine, and Ashley Tianen. "Lunacy in the 19th Century: Women's Admission to Asylums in United States of America." *Oshkosh Scholar*. April 1, 2006. (accessed 2006).

Simpson, Liz. *The Book of Chakra Healing*. New York: Sterling, 1999.

Starsky, Stella, and Quinn Cox. *Cosmic Coupling: The Sextrology of Relationships*. New York: Three Rivers, 2009.

—. *Sextrology: The Astrology of Sex and the Sexes*. New York: HarperResource, 2004.

Index

0

1

2

3

4

5

6

7

8

9

A

B

C

D

E

F

G

S

T